I WAS THERE
by Hans Peter Richter

"From the time the narrator first hears
his father praising Hitler's accomplishments to the day he witnesses his boyhood
friends killed in battle, the taut dramatic
scenes add up to a plausible account of how
it was to be an enthusiastic member of the
Hitler Youth."
              --Kirkus Reviews

I
WAS
THERE

I WAS THERE

by Hans Peter Richter

Translated from the German by Edite Kroll

HOLT, RINEHART AND WINSTON
New York   Chicago   San Francisco

"... and they will never be free again."

Adolf Hitler:
speech of April 12, 1938
in Reichenberg, Sudetenland.

I am reporting how I lived through that time and what I saw—no more. I was there. I was not merely an eyewitness. I believed—and I will never believe again.

Hans Peter Richter

Contents

I WAS THERE

I

-1933-

The Murder

"Germany awake!"

I shot up in bed and listened.

Down in the street two men were arguing—one young and one old, to judge by their voices.

I couldn't make out any words.

Then there were two bangs. Shots!

Hurried steps faded away in the direction of Kranstrasse.

The door to my room opened softly. Mother looked in. When she saw I was sitting up, she came and perched on the edge of my bed.

"What's happening?" I asked.

Mother put her arm around my shoulder; she was wearing a coat over her nightgown. "You wouldn't understand," she whispered. "You're too young! You needn't be afraid."

I felt her uneasiness. "Where is Father?" I asked.

We listened.

Everything was quiet again. But every so often it seemed as if we could hear a suppressed groaning—as if someone was trying to call for help.

Suddenly a heavy car roared around the corner. Brakes shrieked. Many hobnailed boots jumped onto the cobblestones.

Commands echoed through the night. Shortly afterward a second lighter car came racing down the street and pulled to a stop.

A scream rang out.

We didn't dare look out the window.

The second car raced off again with squealing tires.

In the street men were working with dark lanterns, whose light illuminated my room.

Mother's hair hung down in disarray.

The beams of the dark lanterns wandered across the window, casting a shadow like an enormous black cross against the ceiling.

Mother huddled into herself.

I noticed she was shaking.

Her breaths came quickly.

We clung more tightly to each other.

The racket continued for almost an hour. Then the clatter of feet stopped and the heavy car drove off.

Mother stayed with me.

We waited for a long time.

Finally Mother said, "Go to sleep, my boy! I think it's over." She tucked the blanket under my shoulders and left the room without making a sound.

I stayed awake until Father came home.

When I was allowed downstairs the following afternoon, Heinz was doing gymnastics on the gate. "Have you seen it?" he said.

"What?" I asked stupidly.

Heinz climbed down. "I'll show you!" he said, and motioned for me to follow him. He ran ahead. At the corner he turned into Turmstrasse.

People were milling outside the baker's. We squeezed through them and pushed to where we could see.

At the spot where the gutter drainpipe disappeared into the ground, a large wreath leaned against the wall. Its red bow, with the swastika on a white background, lay spread out on the sidewalk. "For our murdered comrade" was written in gold letters on one of its streamers. The other read: "Germany Awake!"

The cry in the night.

Flanking the wreath, two Hitler Youths stood honor watch, their legs spread wide, hands on their gun belts, chin straps tightly fastened. Despite the cool weather they wore only their brown shirts with the swastika armbands around the left sleeves. They stared fixedly ahead, without moving a muscle.

Around them men and women were excitedly discussing what had happened.

"I saw everything!" a little woman declared, gathering the curious around her. "We were already in bed when we heard these shots and. . . ."

All agog, a young girl broke in: "And the murderer? Did you see the murderer, too?"

The little woman shrugged her shoulders regretfully. "He was already gone! Must have been one of those Reds!"

A fat woman scolded: "It's a disgrace! Those good-for-nothing Communists have nothing better to do than shoot each other. It makes one afraid to go out at night!"

Another woman agreed. "Damned politicians! Hitler or Thaelmann—brown or red—what's the difference! It's us who suffer either way!"

An older man disagreed. "But no," he said, polishing his glasses. "It makes a difference whether the Communists or the National Socialists control the government. The Communists want to take away all our possessions—"

Mockingly, the fat woman interrupted him: "Let 'em come! They won't strain a muscle with the little that belongs to me."

The man was about to explain when the woman who hadn't spoken so far turned to him. "Say, you must be getting paid by them," she said, pointing to the two Hitler Youths, "for holding election speeches."

The man pulled in his head and said nothing.

"Reds or browns, they're the same to me," the fat woman went on. "Main thing is we have enough work and enough to eat!"

A boy with a visored cap pushed down low on his forehead grumbled: "The devil take the browns!" He sniffed and spit exactly between the two streamers.

Everyone stood frozen.

The spitter turned and walked away.

Nobody moved. Silently they watched him go.

But then anger erupted. Now all agreed. "Disgraceful! Desecrator! Red! Criminal!" Everyone bleated at the same time. The uproar attracted more curious people.

The seething crowd blocked the street.

"After him!" someone bellowed.

Nobody budged.

Two policemen came down the street on their rounds. "Keep walking! Move along!" they ordered. Calmly and with assurance they cleared first the roadway and then the sidewalk. The crowd scattered.

Only the two Hitler Youths stayed by their wreath. Motionless, they looked as if all this didn't concern them.

"I find it splendid," Heinz said, "how the Hitler Youth behaves itself."

It was already getting dark when the fat woman called to us: "They're looking for the murderer in Kranstrasse!"

At the corner of Kranstrasse people were jammed tight. There were men carrying dinner pails, women with shopping bags, little girls with dolls' carriages, and boys with little brothers who had runny noses.

We noticed Günther not far from us.

Policemen had formed cordons at the entrances to Kranstrasse. Heavily armed, billy clubs at the ready, they stood with linked hands and let nobody in or out. Whenever the crowd got too close to the barricade, the policemen called threateningly: "Stand back! Move along!"

Everyone stayed.

In spite of the orders, more and more people gathered. The cordons tightened themselves.

When the masses swelled so much the cordons threatened to break, a shrill whistle sounded through Kranstrasse.

At once a second detachment of policemen rushed out of a nearby doorway. They positioned themselves behind the first cordons and linked arms, so now there was a double line of policemen blocking the approaches to Kranstrasse.

Because the street dropped off steeply, we could see everything from our spot at the corner.

Kranstrasse itself was empty, except for a lone police van parked in the middle of the roadway. The policemen fanned out around the van were watching the house fronts with rifles at the ready. A strong searchlight mounted on top of the van was trained on the windows and roofs; its beam picked out other policemen who, weapons in hand, were making a house-to-house search.

Excited, we watched their progress. Everyone expected the murderer to be taken into custody momentarily. Everyone wanted to see a murderer.

Whenever the searching policemen stepped out of a house, even the slightest noise ceased. The tension mounted from house to house, from apartment to apartment. Whenever the policemen turned to the next building without a pause, audible disappointment ran through the waiting crowd.

After half of Kranstrasse had been searched without success, the mood lightened. People began to chat, dared to make comments in the darkness.

"Hey, Sergeant! There he goes!" someone called out. And when two police sergeants actually turned around, many people laughed.

The search party was approaching the last house on Kranstrasse. Still the murderer had not been found.

Bystanders started to mock them. "They'll never find him," said one. And another explained in a serious tone: "They *can't*. He's helping with the search!"

Nobody laughed at the joke.

"The Reds got him away long ago!" Heinz whispered to me. "Otherwise the storm troopers would surely have brought him out early this morning."

Günther gave Heinz a searching look.

The policemen left the last house on Kranstrasse. Their leader reported to two higher officers. They were still talking when another whistle sounded shrilly through the street. The rear cordon dissolved. The policemen hurried to the van on the double and got inside. The searchlight was turned off. The men unloaded their weapons.

Another whistle.

The front cordon broke apart; the policemen fell into line.

The van moved slowly off. A sergeant walked ahead and cleared a path for it.

But the people wouldn't think of leaving. They were dissatisfied with the outcome. Some, perhaps, hoped something would still happen; others wanted to watch the men marching off.

At that moment a song rang out behind us. It drowned out the noise of the police van and the chattering of the onlookers.

> "When the golden evening sun
> sent its last rays, its last rays,
> one of Hitler's regiments
> entered a small town."

Everyone turned and watched the singers approach. A whole S.A. *Sturm* was coming up behind us. Their leader was followed by the Nazi flag and three platoons. Most of the S.A. men wore brown shirts and boots; only a few had swastika armbands around their jacket sleeves.

> "Their songs sounded sadly
> through the quiet little town, little town;
> for they carried to the grave
> a Hitler *Kamerad*. . . ."

The police van had stopped to let the S.A. *Sturm* march past. The crowd, held spellbound by the spectacle, refused to clear the roadway.

"Quiet all!" commanded the storm troop leader. In front of the police van he stepped aside—while his storm troopers kept advancing.

"Unit—halt!"

The S.A. men stopped as one.

"Left—turn!"

The company stood facing the police van.

The storm troop leader looked around; he regarded the men in the van.

"At ease!"

The storm troop leader walked toward the police van. The crowd cleared a path for him.

With his right hand raised and a loud "Heil Hitler!" he greeted the old police sergeant. "We would like to hand over the wanted murderer," he said so clearly that everyone could understand him.

The sergeant didn't know how to react. Helplessly he looked around.

"Bring him forward!" the storm troop leader shouted. Two big S.A. men stepped from the last file of the first platoon. In their arms hung a man with torn, blood-encrusted clothes. His face was disfigured from countless blows; his feet scraped over the pavement; he seemed to be unconscious.

"Oh!" moaned some women as the man was dragged past them.

"You sure knocked him around," a man commented.

Horrified, Günther looked at the murderer.

Heinz turned away in disgust.

Two policemen received the unconscious man and bedded him down in the van.

When they started to ask the storm troop leader something, he waved off the question. He walked over to his platoons and immediately marched them off.

At walking speed the police van followed the S.A. *Sturm*.

A police detachment closed the procession.
Heinz and I ran after them.
From a distance we heard the S.A. men singing:

"In the German land we march,
for Adolf Hitler we fight.
The Red brood,
let's beat them to pulp.
Storm troops are on the march.
Attention!
Clear the way!"

Gradually the crowd dispersed in the side streets.
Only Günther stayed close to us.
"There, you've seen it again!" said Heinz. "The Brown Shirts, they know how to get things done!"

The <u>Internationale</u>

I sat with Günther on the front steps of our house. We were waiting for my father. He was due home from work around now. Then Günther would go home and we'd have our evening meal.

It was drizzling. The light was dim. It was cool for summer.

Günther said, "I want to have Heinz for my friend."

"Why shouldn't you?" I asked.

Günther didn't answer.

I tugged at my shoelaces.

All at once Günther began to sing softly: "Arise, ye prisoners of starvation!"

And I fell in: "Arise, ye wretched of the earth."

Together we sang out against the unfriendly weather across the wet street:

> "For justice thunders condemnation
> A better world's in birth...."

Some passersby hastened their steps when they heard us singing; others looked at us and smiled; one old worker winked encouragingly.

Just then my father turned into our street. When he realized the singing came from us, he gestured with his arms and his briefcase and came running toward us as fast as he could. "Boys! Are you crazy?" he called to us as he ran.

Puzzled, we fell silent.

He reached us gasping for breath and ordered: "Get up! Come with me!" He explained nothing.

Günther was still humming the *Internationale* under his breath as he climbed the stairs to our apartment.

Father let us into the apartment. He shut the door firmly and leaned against it. Still short of breath, he called out: "It's me, Mother! I'll be right with you!" In a lower voice he added, "But first I must talk to the boys."

We stood in the dark hallway feeling guilty, but didn't know why. Restlessly we waited for what Father had to say to us.

"Where did you learn the song?" he asked.

I shrugged.

"My father sings it often in the evening—when he's in a good mood," Günther said.

Mother came up to us. "Which song?"

"Just imagine it, Mother," Father said. "The boys were sitting on the front steps belting out the *Internationale*!"

Mother shook her head. "What's that, the *Internationale*?"

Instead of replying, Father hummed the beginning of the song.

"Oh," said Mother. "The Communist song."

"How old are you, Günther?" Father asked.

"Eight."

Father cleared his throat. "So you're both the same age! Listen to me, boys! I don't know how to explain it—you're still too young to understand—but, well, how shall I say it?..."

Mother, already on her way back to the kitchen, turned and said, "Why don't you leave the children out of politics?"

Father said nothing and thought a moment. "Boys," he said. "Times when you could sing such songs in the street are gone. Our new Chancellor, Adolf Hitler, he doesn't like them. He has outlawed the Reds—so it's really better you forget such songs."

After his speech, Father dabbed the sweat from his forehead. "In the end someone denounces you because of a stupid song like this, and we'll all be put into one of those camps." He pressed down the door handle.

"And what shall we sing?" Günther pouted.

"Well, if you *must* sing outside at all, sing 'Raise high the flags.'" Father opened the door of our apartment.

"Well, Günther, time you went home. We'll be having supper."

Günther said good-by. As he went down the stairs, we could hear him softly singing the *Horst Wessel Lied*:

> "Raise high the flags!
> Stand rank on rank together!
> Storm troopers march
> with steady, quiet tread.
> Comrades shot by Reds and reactionaries
> march with us in spirit. . . ."

Mother had already put the meal on the table. There were fried potatoes with belly pork.

Father cut up his pork the way he liked it. He impaled a potato on his fork and looked at me. "You have dangerous friends," he said, "very dangerous friends."

"But these are childish games," Mother put in.

"Dangerous games nevertheless."

Mother got up; she went and brought the big pot of malt coffee to the table.

The doorbell rang.

Mother went to the door.

We listened.
Mother spoke.
A man's strong voice replied.
Firm steps came through the hall.
The kitchen door opened.
"Heil Hitler!" said the man who entered.
Father nodded. "Evening, Paul."

The Election

In January 1933 Adolf Hitler became Chancellor of the German Reich; in February the Parliament building burned; in March there were elections; in April actions against Jews began; in May the unions were dissolved; in June the political parties started dissolving on their own; in July it became illegal to found new parties; in August, vacation time, things were quieter; in September the Nazi "Party Convention of Victory" was celebrated in Nuremberg; in October Germany left the League of Nations—and now, in November, there were more elections.

Mother was looking out the window. "Hmm," she said, "foggy out. And cool, too." She took my thick overcoat out of the closet and put a woolen scarf around my neck. I had to put on my warm cap as well.

Mother, too, wore her warmest clothes.

Then we went off to the school where the votes were to be cast.

Flags and banners lined the way to the school. Black, white, and red flags alternated with swastika flags. The banners read:

"With Adolf Hitler for Peace!"

"Germany demands Equality!"

"The Right to Self-Determination for Germany!"

Posters showed Chancellor Adolf Hitler beside President Field Marshal von Hindenburg.

In the square cars stood ready to drive the old and the infirm to the elections. The drivers were sitting on the running boards, playing cards.

Many people were walking toward the school. The whole town seemed to be on the move.

Father and Mother often had to exchange greetings with people they knew. Mostly it was just a "Good morning" but sometimes Father raised his right hand and shouted a "Heil Hitler!" across the street. Mother merely nodded, but she, too, said, "Heil Hitler!"

At the school innumerable signs and arrows pointed to the gymnasium. If someone hesitated, an S.A. man or a Hitler Youth immediately showed him the right way. Heinz stood in front of the entrance to the gymnasium; he was distributing sheets of paper, pressing a leaflet into the hand of each voter. He did his work conscientiously; whenever several voters approached at the same time, Heinz barred their way until he had dealt with them all.

Because Heinz was wearing a brown shirt, Mother didn't recognize him until he pressed a leaflet upon her. "What are you doing here?" she asked, taken aback.

"I'm one of them now," Heinz told her proudly.

Mother didn't understand. "Of whom?" she asked.

Heinz pointed to his brown shirt, clicked his heels together, pressed his stack of leaflets against his stomach with his left hand, and placed his right hand flat against the seam of his trousers. He explained, "Of the German *Jungvolk,* which is part of the Hitler Youth."

"Is that so?!" Mother said. "And how old are you?"

"I'm ten already."

"Well, well. Take care you don't catch cold in that thin shirt."

Father was reading the leaflet.

"Heinz!" a shout rang across the schoolyard. "Heinz!"

Heinz made a quick turn toward the caller, a man in a brown uniform at the wheel of a large open car. "Here!" he shouted. The man called again: "Come with me!"

"Yes, sir! Coming!" Heinz turned back to us. "Please excuse me, but I must help my father bring in voters." And he again clicked his heels together. Pointing to me with his chin, he said, "He should become a *Pimpf.*"

As Heinz ran to the car and swung himself onto the seat beside his father, Father followed him with his eyes.

The car started off with a jerk, left the schoolyard, and headed toward the suburb.

We entered the gymnasium. An attendant met us and directed me to sit on a bench by the entrance next to other children. We had to stay there until our parents had cast their votes.

Father and Mother joined the line for ballots and envelopes.

Each received two bits of paper, one white, one green.

"What's the good of this?" one man remonstrated. He held up the white ballot. "You can only make an X-mark for Hitler here!" He spoke in a loud voice.

At once all talk stopped; not a sound could be heard; everyone looked at the man.

I recognized him. He was Günther's father.

"And if I don't want to vote for Hitler?" he now asked.

The attendant closed the door to the gymnasium. With a few steps he hurried over to Günther's father.

But Günther's father wouldn't let himself be interrupted. "And this?" he shouted. In a loud voice he began to read from the green ballot:

> "Do you, German man, and you, German woman, endorse the policies carried out by your government, and are you willing to affirm this government as representing your wishes and to solemnly pledge it your support?"

Before Günther's father could read more, the attendant had gripped him by the arm.

Silently, all of us in the gymnasium watched as Günther's father calmly demanded, "Kindly let go of my arm."

"Keep quiet!" warned the attendant. "You are disrupting an election and influencing voters."

Günther's father held out the two ballots to the attendant. "Election?" He laughed. "Kindly show me where one can *choose* on these chits of paper?"

The attendant did not answer.

Slowly, very slowly, Günther's father tore the ballots to shreds in full view of all those present. The shreds fluttered to the floor. Then he allowed the attendant to lead him from the gymnasium.

For a while it was uncannily quiet in the room. But after the attendant had returned alone and opened both wings of the door, everything went on as if nothing had happened. The voters disappeared into the wooden booths, and after a while they reappeared and threw their envelopes into the available ballot boxes.

When I left the gymnasium with my parents, neither spoke. In the schoolyard we met Heinz. He and his father were helping an old woman out of the car. The woman's hands and head were shaking as Heinz carefully led her across the yard. He was explaining to her, "On the white form you must make an X in the circle next to the *Nationalsozialistische Deutsche Arbeiter Partei* and on the green form you must check the yes-circle. Then you will have voted correctly."

Tears came to the eyes of the old woman.

Father took my hand. Back in the street he said to Mother, "A good boy, that Heinz." And he turned to me and said, "You should find friends like him!"

II

-1934-

The March

I pleaded in the morning, I pleaded in the afternoon, I pleaded at night.

But Mother wouldn't budge. "We don't have any money for that!" she declared.

I walked around in despair.

Until Grandmother came for a visit—and bought me the coveted brown shirt.

Now I could take part in the grand military parade after all. The order read: FOR BROWN SHIRTS ONLY! ASSEMBLE SUNDAY 9:00 A.M. AT PARADE GROUND. BRING DAY'S PROVISION.

I slept little the night before. At a quarter to eight I was ready and waiting, my father's old haversack full of food and my shirt fresh and stiff.

When the others arrived in their faded brown shirts, they grinned. But Heinz put a hand on my shoulder and said, "Don't mind them. The main thing is you can be here!" He pointed to my feet. "And don't forget: be sure to keep in step—always." Then he went to join the standard-bearers at the front of our unit.

I mingled with the others.

Nine o'clock.

The oldest platoon leader ordered us to fall in line and count off. "The Brown Shirts of the *Fähnlein* are ready to march off in order!" he reported to the leader of the whole *Fähnlein* (detachment). The leader passed down the ranks. He examined our uniforms, closed a button here, pulled a neckerchief straight there.

I was the smallest.

The leader stopped in front of me, propped his fists on his hips. He inspected me from head to foot, tugged at my collar, and smiled. He smiled a long time. "Ever been on a long march before?" he finally inquired.

"No, sir," I admitted in a faint voice, my dreams dissolving.

"Louder," the leader of the *Fähnlein* demanded, but he went right on to ask another question. "Will you hold out?" he said.

"Yes, sir!" I roared.

But that didn't convince him either. "Well," he decided, "let's hope so."

And finally we moved off, the black banner with the white victory rune at our head. We woke people up with our singing:

The March

"When we march side by side,
singing the old songs,
and when the woods reverberate
we know we will succeed:
A new time is coming with us,
A new time is coming with us."

Yawning men and women with uncombed hair appeared at windows. My fear had dispersed with the singing. Enthusiastically I flung out my legs and swelled my chest, straining the buttons on the new shirt.

As we wheeled from the parade ground into the street, Heinz passed very close to me. He looked at me and nodded.

Not far from the parade ground a lone pedestrian caught up with our unit. Falling into step with us, he marched along beside the *Fähnlein,* swinging his walking stick.

My haversack hung heavy from its strap. With every step I took, its weight reminded me of the march ahead.

We turned into the main street. A streetcar overtook us, ringing its bell. Its few passengers looked down at us.

Staring after the streetcar threw me out of step. I hopped along on my right foot until I found the correct step again.

We were marching toward the center of town.

At a corner, Heinz turned back to me and waved. I waved back and stepped onto the heels of the boy in front, who turned around and gave me a furious look but didn't say anything.

A group of churchgoers crossed our path, dressed in dark clothes. Each was carrying a hymnal. One could see they didn't approve of our march.

But I didn't pay them much attention. I was trying to march in time and avoid stepping onto the boy in front again. I was concentrating hard on watching how he placed his feet and counting under my breath: "Left—two, three, four; left—two, three, four. . . ."

The leader of our *Fähnlein* was circling the unit. He stayed near me a long time, marching behind me for a while and watching me.

I summoned all my strength not to attract his attention. But to no avail. I promptly fell out of step and clumsily stumbled along behind the others.

Suddenly the leader had disappeared. But now Heinz was marching alongside me.

I hadn't noticed his arrival.

Traffic in the street had grown heavier. Several cars now drove along beside the *Fähnlein,* honking their horns. Some drivers and passengers stared at us, while others raced past so quickly the wind whipped our faces.

Gradually I began to feel my legs, began to realize I had slept too little. I grew tired. I no longer tried to march in step. I fell behind a little and made my own pace.

At the center of town there were more people. Singly and in groups they lined the sidewalks.

An old woman shook her head when she noticed me at the end of the unit. I still remember that. Otherwise I was no longer aware of my surroundings. I seemed to float in a cloud of noise and colors, utterly indifferent to everything around me. In front of me marched an army of brown backs, and I had to march, to march. . . .

"Give me your haversack!" Heinz told me and proceeded to unstrap it without waiting for my assent.

At the market square a car with a loudspeaker mounted on it received us. Its march music and announcements drowned out every other sound.

It undid me altogether. Staring blankly in front of me, I kept telling myself: "Stick it out! Don't give up! Stick it out! . . ."

Other *Fähnleins* and units of workers were joining us from all sides. A seemingly endless brown ribbon was running through the streets to the river.

Heinz took a lot of trouble over me. He distracted me, led me by the arm, supported me when I threatened to fall.

People in Sunday clothes streamed beside the undulating line of brown shirts. All were making for the same place.

Things were dancing before my eyes. I saw nothing but legs that raised themselves and legs that lowered themselves, knees that bent and straightened, feet that were raised and feet that stamped. Legs, knees, feet, cobblestones, cobblestones. . . .

At the bridge ramp came the order: "Break step!" Some unpacked sandwiches, others began to tell stories. The even clicking of marching in step turned into a scraping shuffle.

I was now staggering behind my *Fähnlein*.

Heinz linked arms with me. "Here's ten pfennigs," he said. "On the side of the ramp over there is a streetcar stop. Go home. If you step out of the rank here and pretend to tie your shoelaces, no one will notice. I'll tell our leader."

I didn't understand what Heinz was talking about. He simply pushed me onto the sidewalk. "It'll be better next time!" he said consolingly and pressed the haversack into my hand.

I leaned against the bridge rail.

Fähnlein after *Fähnlein* marched past me.

All at once I realized what had happened. Without meaning to I broke into sobs—very quiet sobs, but they shook me.

A woman asked, "Aren't you feeling well?"

I started to run—to the streetcar stop.

The Reception

The sun was beating down on us. We had stood unprotected in the heat for almost four hours.

Across from us nurses were busy with a girl who had fainted.

Together with units of storm troopers, the Hitler Youth,

and the leagues of girls, we were cordoning off a large square.

The air over the empty square was shimmering.

An enormous banner announced: THE PERSON WHO LOVES HIS PEOPLE PROVES IT SOLELY THROUGH THE SACRIFICES HE IS WILLING TO MAKE FOR ITS SAKE!—ADOLF HITLER.

To pass the time, we took turns singing songs. Sometimes the masses of people surrounding us on all sides joined in. In between, the loudspeakers blared out march music.

From time to time someone curious stepped forward and looked down the street to the right.

Nothing! Nothing but people as far as you could see, and in between the human walls just enough room for a car to pass. And flags from every window. A sea of people and flags.

Heinz, too, was bored. He kept stepping from one foot to the other and staring at the ground before him.

Nobody felt like talking.

In shorter and shorter intervals the leader of our *Fähnlein* paced off the cordon. He tried to make our wait easier by whispering different messages like, "Only half an hour to go!" "Can't be long now!" or "He's been reported!" each time around.

Suddenly, totally unexpectedly, we heard it.

At first it was only a murmur, but then it grew, increased in volume. Quickly it spread, grew into a roar. Like a storm it swept closer, rushed up the street in a thunderous roar. The crowds of people began to sway back and forth, started to shove and press forward.

A whistle shrilled.

Following instructions, each of us clasped the wrist of his neighbor. The chain was closed. Here and there the *Fähnleinführer* improved a grip, urged someone to stand firm. Then he walked hurriedly back to his place.

All at once I no longer felt exhausted.

Heinz tightened his grip on my wrist. He raised himself on his toes to be able to see farther.

You could feel the excitement everywhere.

Already enthusiastic shouts of "Heil!" could be heard clearly.

Then I saw them. A long line of large black cars slowly pushing their way forward between the waving and cheering people. Thousands of small swastika flags made of paper were waving in the air.

The noise swelled.

Behind me a woman sobbed with excitement.

A few people began to scream: "Heil!—Heil!"

The first car was forced to a stop.

A groan of disappointment ran through the crowd.

The car started up again.

The voices tumbled over each other, broke.

Ten thousand voices roared: "Heil!"

The large black car rolled onto the empty square.

The chain broke.

Impossible to restrain, the mass of people surged forward.

"Hold fast!" Heinz shouted.

The Reception

My left neighbor let go.

My right hand clamped tighter.

Heinz screamed.

They pushed.

Stomped.

Raged.

"Heil!"—"Heil!"

I teetered.

Heinz pulled me upright.

I was being carried.

Heinz dug his fingers into my wrist.

"Heil!"—"Heil!"—"Heil!"

I whimpered with pain.

Heinz didn't let go.

I pitched forward.

Above me people, feet, uncountable numbers of feet. . . .

"Heil!"—"Heil!"—"Heil!"

Heinz at my side. "Up! *Up!* They'll trample you to death!"

As suddenly as it had begun, the pressure lessened, stopped. Slowly the masses retreated. A double chain of black uniforms drove them back into their allotted space.

"Heil!"—"Heil!" thundered across the square.

Heinz stayed close to me, shielded me.

We allowed no one but the storm troopers to push us. Finally we ended up in the front line.

The square had been cleared.

The black cars drew up beside one another.

"Heil!"—"Heil!" Without end: "Heil!"—"Heil!"

I massaged my wrist while shouting: "Heil!"—"Heil!"
Heinz waved both arms while roaring: "Heil!"—"Heil!"
"Attention!" a voice boomed over the loudspeaker.
Even the old people stood straighter.

"I hereby introduce our *Führer* and Chancellor of the Reich, Adolf Hitler!" bounced back from the houses around the square.

A short man in a brown uniform quickly strode across the square. He stopped short before the largest car and raised his arm in the salute.

"My *Führer!* I wish to report party comrades, members of organizations, and town inhabitants duly assembled!" rang clearly and distinctly across the square.

I looked at Heinz. "But that's. . . ." I whispered.

"My father!" he finished proudly, without looking at me.

The Collection

"Nobody shall go hungry. Nobody shall suffer cold!" proclaimed the man from the *Winterhilfswerk* (Winter Relief Fund). His gloved hands turned up the collar of his brown overcoat.

We drew closer together on our wooden benches, trying to get warm.

The Collection

"So that nobody will suffer want in the German Reich," the speaker continued, "our Führer and *Reichskanzler* Adolf Hitler created this Winter Relief Fund soon after coming into power." He stepped from one foot to the other.

We pushed our hands into our trouser pockets as deep as they would go and huddled in our seats.

"Everyone must make sacrifices!" the man began again. "From the grownups our Führer expects contributions of money and objects. But from you he demands selfless dedication to public collections." He formed a fist with both hands and blew into it.

Heinz rubbed his ears warm.

"Everyone receives a collection box and fifty badges." He held up one of the badges. "For each badge there must be at least—I repeat *at least*—twenty pfennigs in the box. But the more money you collect, the better you will please our Führer."

He stopped for a moment and looked at us searchingly. Then he said, "Are there any questions?"

Otto jumped up from the bench. "I can't collect," he said. "We're visiting my sick grandmother over the weekend."

The man from the *Winterhilfswerk* looked displeased. "So," he said, "your grandmother's sick! And you seriously believe I'll discard the plan of action just because of your grandmother! Too few of you have showed up this evening as it is."

Otto was still standing. "But I'm not allowed to stay home alone!" he protested.

I WAS THERE

The party official picked up a collection box and a cardboard carton filled with badges from the table and pressed both into his hands. "I don't want to hear another word about it!" he said. "I don't care *how* you manage it. We'll settle accounts here on Monday at 6:00 P.M. sharp."

"But we're leaving early tomorrow morning," Otto put in, "and we won't get back till Sunday evening."

The man from the *Winterhilfswerk* took a deep breath. "You must really think I have nothing better to do than worry about your grandmother. Enough is enough! Sign and get out!"

Cowed, Otto signed for receipt of the box and the badges. Then he walked to the door and stood there, holding the tin box with fingers that were numb with cold. He looked as if he was about to cry.

The rest of us crowded around the table to get our things quickly. We wanted to get out of the icy meeting house and home to the warm stove.

When I was ready to go, Heinz touched my arm and said, "Wait, I'll come with you."

Trying to get warm, I ran back and forth between the benches, ran in place, flailed my arms.

Finally Heinz, too, had box and carton. He was one of the last. According to regulations, we reported our departure to the *Fähnleinführer*.

Otto, whose grandmother was sick, still stood by the door. Heinz looked at him and said: "Give 'em to me!" He took both box and carton. "I'll sell the badges for you. And best regards to your grandmother."

"Something to rattle at least!" said Father, and dropped five single pfennigs into my collection box.

With these five pfennigs in my box and my carton full of badges I went onto the street on Saturday afternoon. I didn't dare collect in our neighborhood yet; box and carton hidden beneath my jacket, I ran to the center of town. Here the people strolling past the shop windows were already thinking about Christmas shopping.

In a house entrance I pulled box and carton from their hiding place. I raised the lid of the carton so the badges were visible. Having rattled my pfennigs experimentally once more, I positioned myself in front of a recessed doorway. I resolved to count to three, open my eyes, and address the first grownup who passed. One—two—three.

The young man whose way I blocked already had two badges on the left lapel of his coat. I didn't even rattle my box, but retreated immediately to the doorway.

At least every third passerby was already decorated with badges. The rest looked so grim I didn't have the courage to step in front of them.

Far away, I saw a little woman slowly approaching. She was smiling to herself. She was without a badge.

I determined to start with her.

Ten more steps, five, three—now!

"A small contribution for the *Winterhilfswerk,* please."

Startled, the little woman looked at me. When she understood what I wanted, her face grew stern. With a disdainful gesture she declared, "Already have one!" and hastened her step.

"But. . . ." I wanted to protest, but she had already ducked among the other pedestrians and disappeared.

I was still looking after her when I heard a clattering behind me. Two other boys with collection boxes were approaching, in a pincerlike movement, anyone coming toward them. One would stand to his right, the other to his left, in such a way that the person couldn't walk on. Both would brandish their boxes emphatically until the person they had stopped bought his free passage with a coin. They weren't even offering badges any longer.

I lost all interest in collecting. I was certain I'd never be able to get rid of the fifty badges, that nobody would put money in my box, when an old woman tapped me on the shoulder from behind.

"You still have badges," she said. "Give me one. Otherwise they won't leave me in peace."

I held the box toward her.

She rummaged in her purse. Throwing two ten-pfennig pieces into the collection box, she placed a fifty-pfennig piece in the carton in place of the badge she took out. "For you!" she said.

Disconcerted by so much kindness, I forgot to thank her. I set down the box at a store window while I took the money out of the carton. The window belonged to a bakery, and their crescent rolls cost only five pfennigs apiece. Or you could get sugar pretzels for the same amount.

I felt hungry.

But my box was still almost empty.

Resolutely I threw the fifty-pfennig piece into my box.

Although the box now rattled a bit louder, I didn't sell the badges any faster, or more easily.

I dreaded approaching people.

When I met Heinz, there were still forty-seven badges in my carton.

"How many have you got left?" I asked him.

"Eight!"

"First or second carton?"

"First," Heinz replied. "I'll sell Otto's tomorrow."

"How do you do it?" I inquired.

"It's easy," Heinz began.

"I don't think it's that easy," I said. "I've only sold three in an hour and a half."

Heinz smiled. "Hold these a moment," he said, handing me his box and carton. He took mine instead and immediately steered toward the nearest woman.

The woman already had a badge.

Heinz bowed slightly and smiled. He beamed at her as if she'd promised him a cream tart.

And the woman smiled back. She stopped, put her hand in her pocketbook, and handed Heinz a fifty-pfennig piece. She only accepted one badge in exchange and even thanked Heinz.

I watched open-mouthed. I was amazed. I was so full of admiration that I forgot to do any collecting myself. When Heinz returned, he had sold three badges. And I— I hadn't even rattled his box.

"That's how you must set about it," Heinz said.

We exchanged boxes and cartons.

"You stay here!" he ordered. "I'll go to another street so we won't snatch customers from each other."

Otto was waiting for Heinz outside the door to our *Heim,* our meeting house. He was anxiously walking up and down. "What's keeping him?" he asked me.

I didn't know.

This time the place was heated.

The man from the Relief Fund was sitting behind the table. In front of him stood a stack of counting boards. With a pair of pliers he'd snip off the seals of the collection boxes, fling the little pieces of wire to the floor, rip off the lids, and tip the contents onto the counting boards. We had to build our coins into towers while he watched.

Then he'd compute the results and enter the figures on a list beside our names. Whenever he had to take back badges, he'd grumble.

I had sold everything and my box contained three marks and twenty pfennigs more than I had to have. I was content. Not so the man from the *Winterhilfswerk*. He grumbled.

He poured the counted coins into a little sack, bundling up the paper money and placing it on top.

Finally Otto came into the *Heim*. He looked serious. His box was wedged under his arm.

"Well, how's the sick grandmother?" the man from the Relief Fund greeted him with a grin. "Did she buy a badge, too?"

"No," Otto replied. "She's being buried on Wednesday."

For a short moment everything was quiet in the room. We all stared at Otto, who was handing his box over to the man without looking at anyone.

"You did well," the man stated after he had emptied the box.

Otto said nothing.

"Why all this now?" the man asked. He stood up. "If you hadn't collected for the fund, your grandmother would still have died. This way you learn how to grow hard, as the *Führer* wants you to."

"There's my box to go still!" Heinz interrupted in a loud voice. He banged his box down onto the table.

Distracted, the speaker sat down again and opened the last box.

While Otto built up his coin towers, no one spoke.

The man from the *Winterhilfswerk* sat brooding at his place.

The leader of our *Fähnlein* walked up to Otto and stood behind him, putting his hand on his shoulder.

We huddled silently and waited for the final results.

At last the moment arrived.

While the man from the Relief Fund gathered up his things, our leader picked up the list and read out the amounts collected. To make it exciting, he read the worst results first and left the best till the end.

I stood in seventh to last place.

The winner was Otto with his dead grandmother.

-1935-

The School Ceremony

"Well, you've heard enough about the Saar," said the teacher. "I don't know more myself right now."

We leaned back in our benches.

The teacher slowly pulled a pipe from his pocket. "But we're still early." Reverently he filled the pipe bowl and set fire to the tobacco.

"Only a quarter of an hour to go." The whisper ran through the class from behind.

Puffing at his pipe, the teacher sat on a pupil's desk in the front row and looked across the benches.

Almost everyone wore a brown shirt. Only three or four had come in their Sunday suits.

"When I see you dressed like that, I want to tell you something," the teacher began.

We looked at him expectantly. For a long moment it was very quiet in the classroom.

The teacher took a few puffs, then he began: "My father was a tailor here in town. He earned just enough to feed his family. But still he paid for me to go to high school, because he hoped I'd have a better life one day. I didn't always please my father, and it sometimes must have seemed to him that the school fee had been wasted. I know that now, though I didn't then."

No one made a sound. All listened, motionless.

The teacher held a match to his tobacco. When the tobacco was lighted once more, he went on: "As a tailor my father knew a lot about fabrics. He once advised me to buy only suits made of the best English cloth. I have followed this advice until now."

The teacher got off the desk and in long strides walked slowly up and down between the benches.

We followed his journey through the classroom with our eyes, trying not to make the slightest sound that might distract him from his story.

"For a teacher with my salary that hasn't been easy," he now went on. "But so far I haven't regretted my decision. I'd like to stick to it as long as possible—if only because of my father. Yes—and brown cloth such as you are wearing—that isn't made in England."

He knocked out his pipe in the flowerpot, keeping his back turned to us as he did so.

We waited patiently until he turned around again.

"That's all for today!" He put his pipe away. "Up!" When we stood, he saluted with raised arm: "Heil Hitler, boys!" With a wave of his hand he dismissed us. "Go on down, the bell will ring any moment now."

We stormed out of the classroom.

As I passed the teacher, he held me back by the shoulder.

"So that I won't forget," he said, "please make my apologies to the principal. Say I regret I'm unable to attend the ceremony, that I'm prevented from doing so for personal reasons."

We had just reached the courtyard when the bell rang.

The flagpole in the center of the yard was almost twice as high as the sickly trees growing along the sides. The swastika banner hung slack.

The school janitor was still drawing chalk squares on the ground, marking the places where the classes were to stand, when the principal came out of the building.

Behind him the classes spilled out into the yard. All ran immediately to their prescribed positions and stood at attention. The Brown Shirts stood in front. Behind them hid those in Sunday suits. There were about three or four in each class.

In the neighboring class Günther was the only one to break the uniform brown with his green suit.

We had to stand at attention. Our ranks were dressed. We were reported. Then the ceremony began.

The principal smoothed the brown jacket over his

stomach. "Comrades," he began. "I have asked you to assemble here today to celebrate a truly memorable event. You have all either heard it over the radio or read it in the newspaper: the Saar has returned its allegiance to our German Fatherland. The ignominious, so-called 'Peace' Treaty of Versailles severed the Saar region from the German Reich. Our sworn enemy, France, seized it. But the Germans of the Saar have shown the French where they belong. They didn't rest until they made it clear to those robbers that the Saar always was German, is German, and will remain German. An overwhelming majority of 91 out of every 100 voters want the Saar to be returned to Germany. The people from the Saar want to come home to the Reich."

Some stared at the sky, bored.

At first the teachers, who wore brown and were assembled behind the principal, glowered at everyone who seemed inattentive. But the longer the speech lasted, the more they, too, relaxed.

"And whom can we thank for this?" the principal continued, looking at the boys in the front row. "Whom else but our beloved Führer, Adolf Hitler! It is he who will release us from the shackles of the infamous Versailles Treaty. He has already taken the first step, and believe me, comrades, more will follow."

Safe from the eyes of the principal, boys began to chatter in the back rows. Even the teachers were whispering and smiling behind their principal's back.

"It saddens me," the principal was saying, "when I see

how little gratitude we show our great leader who is in the process of raising the German Reich to its true glory and heroic greatness. I will feel no real pleasure until only Brown Shirts surround me, until all the opponents of the Führer have been wiped out!" He pointed to Günther's class and went on, "Look how the uniform picture of one whole class is destroyed by one boy, the only one who has not found himself willing to join our supreme leader. It is a disgrace for our school. I feel ashamed each time I remember that there are still boys in my school who do not unreservedly proclaim their loyalty to the Führer, boys who do not belong to the *Jungvolk* or the Hitler Youth. I feel *ashamed!*" he shouted in a plaintive voice.

Günther stood at the back of his class with bowed head.

Others were moving away from him.

In the other classes, too, boys were suddenly moving away from those wearing Sunday suits.

The principal then announced that there would be neither school nor homework for the rest of the day. We concluded the ceremony with the *Deutschlandlied* and the *Horst Wessel Song*.

Delighted at the free afternoon, we ran home.

Günther walked home alone.

And I had forgotten to deliver my teacher's apologies.

The Book

We were waiting on the stairs. Some were squatting, others stood around.

I leafed through the book from which we were going to read, showing around the drawings to the stories.

Upstairs, by the door to our *Heim,* Heinz was arguing. "Today is Wednesday," he was saying, "and on the duty roster for Wednesday it says '*Heim* evening.' We want to read aloud, so let us in!"

But the new leader of Platoon Number 1 barred his way. "I'm having an important conference with the leader of a girls' platoon," he explained. "I need the room for that. If you insist on indoor duty go across the hall. There's another room."

Heinz said, "The second platoon's already there, and they don't have room for us, too. Besides, this is our room."

Angry now, the platoon leader of the *Jungvolk* said, "I will not relinquish this room. As far as I am concerned, you can do outdoor duty with your squad."

Heinz refused. "What could we do outside in this weather?"

Impatiently, the platoon leader declared: "Go to the parish house and annoy the *Neudeutsche.*"

"Is that the best you can come up with?" jeered Heinz. "Why on earth should we bother the Catholic kids?"

"How dare you speak to me like that!" the platoon leader angrily declared. "Enough of this! I have neither the time nor the inclination to chatter with you here on the stairs. Prove that you are men, soldiers like those the

Führer needs for the *Wehrmacht!*"

"We are members of the *Jungvolk,* not soldiers!" Heinz demurred.

"Cowards is what you are!" scolded the platoon leader. "Listen. I am hereby giving you an order: You and your squad are to go at once to the parish house. There you will provoke the Catholic youths to infractions. Is that clear? I will personally check on the execution of my order. Dismissed!" And he banged shut the door to our *Heim.*

Before it shut completely, we heard the giggle of the girl leader.

"Put the book away," said Heinz as he came down the stairs.

"Don't be silly!" said one boy. "We can sit in the waiting room at a streetcar stop and read there."

Heinz shook his head. "Didn't you hear," and he imitated the voice of the platoon leader, "I will personally check on the execution of my order!"

"We're the ones who'll get the beating, not him," someone muttered.

Outside a fine drizzle fell. Small puddles had formed in the alley. Only a few pedestrians were pushing themselves along the house walls to their destinations.

We crept in a line through the Turmstrasse, making use of any overhang. The last boys straggled behind listlessly.

The book beneath my jacket, I trotted silently beside Heinz.

The Book

At the *Turmplatz* we all squeezed together into a small but roofed-over recess to protect us from the rain. Then we debated how best to provoke the boys in the parish house.

The parish house stood across from the church, a rear building you could get to only through a covered gateway. I was chosen to look the situation over.

As I crossed the *Turmplatz,* I ran into Günther. He was walking up and down in front of the gateway, his hands buried deeply in the pockets of his raincoat, his cap pulled down over his ears. He nodded to me and looked puzzled when I disappeared into the entranceway.

My steps sounded muffled beneath the gateway. No one stopped me. Unhindered, I penetrated as far as the church courtyard. No guards or monitors lurked anywhere, although there had to be many boys inside the parish house. The window catches hung full of raincoats. One boy was even sitting on the window ledge. I had seen enough!

I ran back to the gateway.

Günther was still standing outside it.

I waved to the others.

Günther watched them hurry—singly and with care—across the square to the gateway, where they gathered around me.

The square was empty, except for one old woman who was lugging home a heavy net shopping bag full of groceries.

Günther noticed her, walked over to her, and helped her carry the groceries.

Heinz was the last to arrive at the gateway. He handed

the book back to me. Mumbling crossly to himself, he positioned us as in choir practice, facing the parish house. Quietly he counted: "One, two three!"

And we belted out:

> "Open the windows, open the doors!
> Watch who comes running in a jogtrot,
> unwashed and uncombed,
> a *PX* on his shirt—"

That's as far as we got.

"Backs against the wall!" bellowed Heinz.

Then they were on top of us.

No way out of the yard!

Caught!

And they walloped us.

I couldn't see anything at all any more, but from time to time I heard slapping sounds.

Gasps!

Groans!

I punched, kicked.

And I took a lot of blows.

It was over as suddenly as it had begun.

One boy's nose was bleeding; another was badly bruised; one boy limped, and another was crying because he had fallen into a dirty puddle.

A scratch went right across Heinz's face from forehead to chin. He was guiding a boy who was stumbling about in the gateway with outstretched arms, searching for his glasses.

I was missing a fistful of hair and all my ribs ached.

"Come on!" Heinz said, depressed. "Let's go home."

"A pity the new platoon leader wasn't with us," someone muttered. "I sure wouldn't have begrudged him the beating!"

I looked back one more time.

Günther still stood by the gateway. His raincoat had a rip in it I hadn't noticed earlier.

In the street in front of the gateway lay the book we had meant to read aloud—torn to shreds.

The Jew

The others clattered down the stairs.

Heinz ordered me to tidy up the room. Then he left, too.

I straightened overturned benches, pushed tables back to their places, wiped the smeared blackboard, swept up scraps of paper, and was the last one to head for home.

Outside it was already beginning to get dark.

Some stores had their lights on. I wandered slowly past the illuminated and dark windows, stopping to look from time to time. I heard noises coming from Kranstrasse.

When I got closer, I could make out boys' voices, voices

that yelled and whistled, shouted and laughed; sometimes they even sounded as if they were singing.

From the corner I could see everything.

Our squad was letting loose. They were hooting and dancing around in the middle of the street. Their uniforms looked black in the gathering darkness. Whenever a face came into the circle of light from the street lantern, it shimmered greenish-yellow.

Someone stood in the middle of their ring.

"Dirty Jew!" echoed from the house walls. "Dirty Jew!"

From a distance, from doorways and windows, grown-ups looked on. No one intervened.

I walked closer.

"Stinking Jew!" a boy in the circle began.

At once the others fell in and bellowed in unison: "Stinking Jew! Stinking Jew!"

In the center of the ring a boy held his hands before his face. He wore not a uniform, but a dark jacket. His hair—

I knew that jacket and that hair; it was Friedrich! Friedrich from our house!

One of his tormentors jostled him.

He stumbled, seemed about to fall, caught himself.

A kick.

Resigned, Friedrich put up with it all. He didn't move, and shielded only his face.

Slowly I drew back. I tried to duck into a doorway.

"Dirty Jew! Stinking Jew!" they jeered. Friedrich hunched his shoulders.

One of the circle had seen me. "Come on!" he called.

"Pig Jew!" one boy shouted. The others promptly joined in: "Pig Jew! Pig Jew! . . ."

One boy leaped forward, grabbed my hand and tried to pull me into the circle. "Join us!" he yelled.

I resisted. "Where is Heinz?" I asked.

"Don't worry about *him*. Heinz is at home. Come on!"

"Why don't you let him be," I said quietly, nodding toward Friedrich.

The other boy stood still. He looked me up and down. Then he spit on the ground in front of me and sneered: "Why don't you slink home to Mummy!" With a gesture full of contempt, he turned back to the circle and hollered: "Dirty Jew! Pig Jew!"

Quickly I retreated to the shadow of the doorway.

"You cowardly dogs!" suddenly resounded through Kranstrasse. Günther! His fists hammering, he threw himself into the circle and stood next to Friedrich.

The screaming broke off. Everyone stared in astonishment at this new arrival.

"You rotten cowards!" Günther screamed.

This stoked their fury. Hands formed into fists.

Günther taunted them. "You lowly scum!"

They edged closer to him.

Friedrich still didn't dare look up.

"You skunks!" Günther's voice broke.

They pressed closer and closer. The closest grabbed his sleeve.

Günther didn't stop shouting.

At that moment an older man walked up to the group. "Aren't you ashamed?" he asked calmly, looking at each of the uniformed boys in turn.

Undecided, they remained where they were.

The old man put his arms around Günther and Friedrich and pulled them to him. He led them both out of the circle. Then he turned back and commanded the others: "Go home!"

IV

-1936-

Packs of Cigarettes

Some had been waiting since morning.

We from the *Jungvolk* and the Hitler Youth were in uniform. This time we all wanted to be part of it.

Günther, too, had come. Hands in the pockets of his jacket, he kept in the background.

We stood and stared across at the other embankment. But we saw only people, people waiting as we were waiting.

More and more people were arriving. Soon they lined the approach several rows deep.

They're coming!

Everyone started to move.

Many a spectator, who had defended his place in the

front row for hours, suddenly found himself behind a wall of backs, thrust back against the guardrail of the bridge.

Günther was pushed closer to us. But he paid no attention to us. He, too, was watching the other side, the direction which they had to come from.

Still they didn't come!

Yet no one was bored. People everywhere were in a good mood.

"At last—German soldiers in the Rhineland again!" someone in the background declared effusively.

Many repeated approvingly, "German soldiers!"

And suddenly they were there!

At their head rode a captain with a steel helmet, his gray battle tunic decorated with flowers. Even his horse had flowers stuck in its bridle. The captain was waving and smiling. The soldiers following behind him stepped briskly and were laughing.

More flowers had appeared from somewhere. Little girls carried clothes baskets filled with snowdrops, violets, daisies, all bound into small bouquets.

The soldiers stretched out their hands, and a shower of bouquets poured over them. Girls and young women ran among the rows and fastened them to the battle-dress tunics of the marchers. Buttonholes and gun belts were soon decorated with flowers.

An older woman pressed a shopping bag full of cigarettes into Heinz's hands. "Throw, boys, throw!" she requested. "To our soldiers!" She took a handful of packs herself and distributed them indiscriminately.

Packs of Cigarettes

Next to Günther stood a little girl with pigtails holding a basketful of flowers. She would point at a particular soldier and Günther would aim at him. Günther never missed; every single bouquet reached the right soldier.

Heinz and I tried to throw our cigarettes into the body of the troops. We didn't want just the outer rows of marchers to get the presents.

A corporal stretched out his hands.

I hurled a pack.

Missed!

The cigarettes fell to the ground.

Before the corporal could bend down, the hobnailed boots of the soldier behind him had crushed the pack.

Heinz tried to do better. But his pack of cigarettes landed among the spectators on the other side of the street.

We tried even harder.

Hopeless!

The fifth or sixth pack of cigarettes hit an innocent bystander in the eye.

Günther, on the other hand, effortlessly got his flowers where he wanted them to go—into open hands.

"And to think it's much harder to throw flowers," grumbled Heinz.

"He sure has the knack!" someone said.

"He does know how," Heinz agreed, his voice sounding a little disappointed.

For a while longer we wondered what to do.

"Too bad about the cigarettes!" Heinz said when we got ready to try again. He took the shopping bag and hurried across to Günther. "You do it!" he said. "Your aim's better."

Günther nodded and took turns throwing flowers and cigarettes to the soldiers.

Heinz and the girl with pigtails held the bag and basket for him.

Preliminary Selection

Olympic fever had gripped everyone. People everywhere spoke only of the Olympic Games that were to be held in Berlin later that summer. Even those for whom sports hadn't existed until now suddenly began to talk about performance and results and skill—in hammer-throwing, the long jump, the hundred-meter run. They knew all the rules and the names of the world and regional champions.

Our town had scheduled a large sports contest for its youth. The best from every school were to participate. Prizes beckoned the winners, and a chance to participate in the statewide contests.

We had almost three weeks to prepare before the contestants from our school would be chosen. Our competitive spirit had been awakened; everyone wanted to take part.

Preliminary Selection

We trained in the morning and during our lunch break; we practiced in the evening and on the way to school; we practiced in class and trained during our free periods; we trained on the way home and in the street; we were still training as we got ready for bed; we practiced. . . .

Even those who knew for sure they wouldn't be selected for the town contest practiced.

Everyone went on hoping, hoping to at least reach the final elimination round.

We guessed which of us were certain to be representing the school at the *Sportsfest*. Among them were Heinz and Günther. Heinz was thought to be one of the best gymnasts on the horizontal bar, and Günther was considered the fastest runner in our age group.

The day of the trials finally arrived. A glorious day! The sun shone in a cloudless sky.

Our school was decorated as if for a festival. The janitor had pulled the tubs of laurels to the entrance and unfurled the swastika flag.

In the schoolyard tracks had been measured out and all the necessary equipment put up, including the horizontal bar. It was fastened between two trees and anchored in the ground. The schoolyard looked like a miniature sports field.

We assembled by class in our gym clothes.

The school principal gave a speech. He started with the games in Greek Olympia and ended with the trials for our town's sports contest.

Afterward the physical education teacher announced the rules of the contests. Because we knew them, we hardly listened. Impatiently we waited for the contests to begin.

The teacher was explaining: "Obviously only those boys can take part in the final contests who belong to the *Jungvolk* or the Hitler Youth and who own uniforms. We have to insist on that if only because of the uniform clothing. What kind of an impression would our delegation make if it were to assemble with each competitor wearing a different-colored suit? No! We will appear in closed formation—in brown shirts! Through donations we have at our disposal a sum of money which will enable us to outfit poor but worthy *Pimpfs* or Hitler Youths. They may report to the school principal at the end of these tryouts."

Günther didn't even bother to participate in the gymnastic tryouts. He was assigned to assist at the horizontal bar.

The contests began simultaneously on all the equipment and at all the tracks.

As school champion, Heinz was allowed to be the first to perform on the horizontal bar.

The gym teacher looked on.

Heinz did an upward circle forward.

The gym teacher nodded approvingly.

Heinz got ready to do a reverse circle. He succeeded effortlessly.

But the bar swayed a little, back and forth.

Heinz repeated the exercise.

The horizontal bar loosened some more in the mooring. Heinz did not notice.

The gym teacher placed his foot on top of the slackening cable.

Once more Heinz swung himself into the air.

The fastening gave way.

The cable slipped.

The bar wobbled.

Günther leaped forward.

Heinz's feet struck his face.

He grabbed both Heinz's legs, held on tight.

Helplessly, Heinz dangled from the swaying bar.

Only now did Günther release his legs. His nose was bleeding. He ran quickly into the school building.

Slowly the gym teacher recovered from his shock. "You sure were lucky, Heinz," he said.

"If it hadn't been for Günther. . . . A pity he isn't one of us!"

The Newcomers

An icy wind whipped across the parade ground. It ripped the smoke from the chimneys of surrounding houses into wisps of gray. A few windows were still covered with ice flowers. People who had to go out bundled up; others stayed at home.

We huddled in the wind shelter offered by a soda stand at the edge of the square. None of us wore a coat and only one owned gloves. Our ears and noses ached from the cold; our frozen red hands were clenched into fists. We stamped from one foot to the other without stopping.

At the far side of the square stood another group of boys wearing thick overcoats. They kept their hands buried deep in their pockets, their woolen caps pulled down low over their ears. From time to time they stamped around in a circle, one behind the other.

"What kind of bunch are they?" someone asked.

No one answered.

"If I didn't have to, I wouldn't be so dumb as to stand around out here!" remarked another.

Suddenly the boys in overcoats looked across at us. There were five of them. One of them was pointing at us.

"What's up with them?" growled the boy with gloves. "Are they looking for a fight?"

Otto rubbed his ears and said, "Not a bad idea! Would warm us up!"

But the other boys in my *Jungvolk* unit didn't care for the suggestion. They were too cold to fight.

So I could move around a little I said, "I'll go and see if anyone's coming."

The others only grunted.

"Get a look at those guys over there at the same time!" one boy suggested. I ran off as fast as I could round the parade ground, looking in turn down all the streets that ran into the square. But I couldn't see any leaders of the *Jungvolk* anywhere.

The boys in overcoats watched my progress around the square. I ran past them especially close.

Günther was one of the five.

We nodded to each other.

I completed the round. "I saw none of ours!" I reported behind the shack.

"What about those over there?" one boy asked.

"Boys from the neighborhood," I replied. "Günther from my school's one of them. But none of ours!"

The boy with the gloves asked, "What are they doing on our parade ground?"

I shrugged. "I don't know. They didn't tell *me*."

After that our conversation died down again. We pressed closer against the wooden wall of the soda stand and watched white smoke coming out of our noses with every breath we took.

The cold got worse.

"I don't care," Otto announced. "And never mind the uniform. I'm going to stick my hands in my trouser pockets."

We muttered in agreement and followed his example.

"Why do they keep us waiting extra long in this damn cold?" complained the boy with the gloves in a plaintive voice. "I'm going to run to the clock at the watchmaker's, and if it's a quarter of an hour past time, I'm going home! Let them start on time!"

But before he had returned from the watchmaker's, the leader of our *Fähnlein* appeared. He was accompanied by his deputies.

Smiling and rubbing his hands, he ordered us to fall in line.

We dragged ourselves from our cover and took up our positions, chattering in the cold.

The deputies assumed their positions.

Because of the weather, our leader didn't bother to check the alignment; he didn't even reprimand us for placing our hands as fists against our trouser seams instead of laying them flat. But after he had taken a count of our shivering handful, he asked in horror, "Is that all? Must have been too cold for the others!" Then he went on, "They still haven't realized that service in the *Jungvolk* is as much of a duty as school attendance. Tell those who stayed home that I can always have them brought to duty by policemen!"

A few mumbled, "Yes, sir!" It was too cold to open one's mouth properly.

The leader looked at us. Then he said, "And none of the new ones have shown up either, eh?"

We looked at each other in astonishment. What new ones? We didn't know anything about new ones!

Only the deputies were nodding meaningfully to each other. The leader looked around. His eyes slid across the parade ground to the boys in overcoats. "Who are they?" he inquired, looking at us while pointing backward with his thumb.

We shrugged.

The boys he had pointed to were staring at us, open-mouthed.

"Otto!" the *Fähnleinführer* called out.

Otto jumped to attention with a start.

"Go and run across. I want to know who they are!"

Otto lumbered across the square and returned at once. "They are the new ones!" he gasped.

"They are the ones!" our leader said. "Otto, quick-march! Go and tell them to get over here, *if* they please!"

Otto made a face. Then he trudged once more across the square, puffing veritable clouds before him. He started waving to the group of boys while he was still running.

But they waited for him to get closer. They discussed something with him and finally they sauntered casually toward us.

Blowing on his fists, the *Fähnleinführer* paced back and forth, back and forth.

We huddled more into ourselves to better withstand the cold. Each hid behind the other to get better cover from the wind.

The others finally arrived. Hands in coat pockets, they walked up to the *Fähnleinführer,* their faces closed, their lips pressed tightly together. Only one removed his cap and said: "Good day!"

We laughed.

Otto reported over the heads of the newcomers: "Command duty executed!" and went back to his place in the rank.

Something was bound to happen.

Because of the tension, I forgot to feel cold. None of us had ever behaved like that. I could already hear the roar of our *Fähnleinführer*.

He had also pressed his lips together. Snorting like a horse, he took such a deep breath his chest curved outward. He began calmly and quietly: "So you are the new ones?!"

Pause.

"A pleasure to meet you!" he continued, and held out his hand.

They took their hands out of their pockets reluctantly. Obviously they mistrusted him.

He shook hands with Günther last.

And Günther declared loudly: "We have no reason to be pleased. We are only here because we must be!"

Our eyes leaped to the leader—and back to Günther. Back and forth.

Günther and the *Fähnleinführer* still stood hand in hand.

Everyone was looking—and waiting.

But the *Fähnleinführer* said nothing in reply. He pressed Günther's hand once more and addressed the new ones generally. "Stand at the end of the line," he said. "We'll march to our *Heim*. It's warmer there."

We were very proud of our new *Heim*. It stood on one of the most beautiful spots in our part of town, close to the park. The Hitler Youth, the *Bund Deutscher Mädel* (League of German Maidens), the *Jungmädel* (Young

Maidens), and the *Jungvolk* could all do their duty there simultaneously. Each unit had a business room and a large room for indoor duty. Wide windows and pale furniture made the rooms light. Books stood on wall shelves in easy reach of everybody. Parlor games lay in open cupboards; table-tennis tops were propped up in the corner. We had a fully equipped workshop in the cellar, as well as showers. A caretaker couple looked after the cleaning and the heating.

Many found the new *Heim* nicer than home.

One could see even the new ones liked the *Heim*.

To begin with, our leader gave a short speech. He spoke of the gratitude German youth owed the Führer for having taken up their cause like no one before him. (With a sweeping wave of his hand he encompassed the room we were sitting in.) As a sign of that gratitude we must at all times prove ourselves worthy of belonging to the youth of the Führer. The Führer expected his youth to be strong, loyal, brave, and clean.

While the *Fähnleinführer* spoke, we watched the new ones. Uninterested, they were looking out the window and didn't seem to be listening.

Finally the leader spoke to each newcomer separately. He said to Günther: "You showed courage back there on the parade ground. Now answer one question, please. Why haven't you joined the *Jungvolk* before now?"

Hesitantly, Günther stood up. Then he looked fully at the *Fähnleinführer* and said calmly, "You imprisoned my father because he's against Hitler."

Our leader swallowed, disconcerted. Then he said, "Surely

he must have *done* something as well; otherwise he wouldn't have been punished?"

Günther nodded. "Yes," he said. "At a meeting my father openly said he didn't believe in Hitler."

The *Fähnleinführer* bit down on his lower lip. He was careful not to ask any more questions. Instead he explained to all what service in the *Jungvolk* meant. Then he had their names entered in various lists and assigned them to different sections of his unit.

Heinz asked for Günther. And Günther was assigned to our squad.

After we had sung a song, we were allowed to go home.

At the door the *Fähnleinführer* stopped Günther. "If ever you have any difficulties, come to see me!" he said, and pushed him through.

On the way home Günther declared, "At least I'm glad I belong to your squad."

U

-1937-

War Games

We marched to the works.

"Works" was the name given to a large area outside of town. Someone had at one time started to build vast factory halls there. But the work had been broken off and the tract of land had lain fallow ever since. Mounds of earth, excavated pits, all were overgrown with grass and underbrush, in between lay piles of stone, remnants of walls, broken train tracks. A perfect spot for war games!

Our *Fähnleinführer* ordered us to stop and break ranks.

We were trying to examine the area more closely when he ordered us to line up again, in two ranks this time. This took longer because everyone had to search for his place.

When we were finally assembled, each rank had to move ten steps away from the other.

I found Heinz in my rank on the left, Günther opposite in the one on the right.

Our leader pulled two large balls of wool from his pocket, one red and one blue.

Our side got the red ball.

Heinz tore the wool into short threads. And everyone tied a thread around his left arm.

Günther looked over to us. He still held his piece of blue thread in his hand. When the *Fähnleinführer* turned away, Günther immediately slipped across to us. "I want to stay with you!" he begged.

But the blues were already complaining. "The reds have one more man than we do. Günther has deserted!"

Günther refused to go back. When the blues tried to get him he resisted.

They turned to the leader.

"Take another in exchange!" he told them.

The blues chose Otto. They didn't even have to argue with him. Otto quickly exchanged his wool thread for Günther's and changed sides, smirking. The blues were delighted because Otto was stronger than Günther.

Some of ours grumbled at the loss.

The leader pretended not to notice and assigned each team its starting position. He and two platoon leaders were going to be referees.

We reds cowered behind a mound of earth. We elected Heinz our leader.

Heinz developed a plan of attack and assigned us. He

named Günther his runner; I was detailed to the scouting patrol.

At the sound of the *Fähnleinführer's* whistle the "battle" began.

I sneaked out and slowly worked my way from bush to bush, creeping along on fingers and toes for better cover. I avoided making any noise and covered the longest stretch on my stomach. But no matter how hard I scouted, I could not discover a single blue. I saw our *Fähnleinführer* talking to the platoon leaders on top of a nearby hill—but nothing else. Behind a piece of wall I straightened up part way and was examining the field before me through a gap between two bricks when I felt a jerking at my left arm. I turned around quickly.

On the ground behind me knelt one of the blues. He held my torn red wool thread out toward me and declared: "You are dead!"

I was the first casualty of the battle.

All those killed in action had to evacuate the battlefield immediately. As I was leaving the field, the blues stormed forward.

My side immediately counterattacked. Heinz ran at their head shouting: "Hurrah! Hurrah!"

Günther followed close behind, also screaming: "Hurrah! Hurrah!"

Deployed over a wide area, the reds ran behind Heinz and Günther bellowing their "Hurrah! Hurrah!"

Suddenly Heinz stumbled and disappeared into a pit.

But the reds couldn't be stopped. They leaped across their fallen leader into hand-to-hand combat with the blues. Only

Günther stayed with Heinz. He knelt down and tried to help Heinz out of the hole.

But the blues had other plans. A small group had cleared a path to one side of the melee and managed to get behind the reds' lines without their noticing. Otto was a member of this group.

At the last moment Günther recognized his enemies. He left Heinz to scrabble for himself and stood protectively before the pit. It was his role to defend the leader of the reds and save him.

But Otto and his companions paid no attention to Heinz; they fell upon Günther.

Günther tried to defend himself.

Two grabbed him.

Günther tried to break away.

They threw him to the ground.

Günther thrashed with his feet.

One sat on his legs.

Günther tried to fling himself around.

While the others held Günther and took care not to harm his red thread, Otto started to thrash him. He thrashed him until Heinz had managed to climb out of the pit. Only when Heinz jumped to his aid did Otto tear Günther's thread and try to flee with the rest of his group.

Günther didn't even try to get up.

But Heinz got hold of Otto and a hard fight began. Each was out to grab the other's thread while saving his own. The two rolled across the ground.

The fallen soldiers gathered curiously around the fighters.

Gradually Otto gained the upper hand.

Heinz began to flag.

But then two reds came to his aid and rendered Otto harmless. Heinz again assumed the leadership.

The battle continued.

Harmoniously the war dead walked over to where I was standing.

"That beating you got because you're always running after Heinz," Otto told Günther.

The Spear

It was already getting dark.

Our tents were standing, pegged down firmly, strewn with fresh straw. The canvas was stretched tight. Tired from the train trip, from the approach march, and from the unfamiliar work, we sat in a circle around the campfire.

I looked across the flames into the setting sun as it sank, enormous, behind the mountains. All I could make out of the village were the light spots made by the whitewashed houses. The woods behind me grew into a seemingly impenetrable wall.

All around us was silence.

Heinz was sitting cross-legged, leaning back against the flagpole. He was telling stories.

But no one listened carefully. One after the other, we

began to yawn. Many were dozing. A few were staring at the night landscape.

Otto was conversing with his neighbor by signs. Günther was forming grass blades into letters.

"Must be almost ten o'clock! Bedtime," Heinz concluded.

We all sighed with relief.

"But before we go into our tents," Heinz began again, "we must detail sentries."

"Oh hell!" Everyone sounded disappointed.

Heinz ignored them. "All by ourselves in a strange place we have no choice but to post sentries. In the first place, it's useful training for our military service, and in the second, a wild boar might root out our pegs during the night and bury us beneath our tents."

One boy in the circle asked: "And how will we protect ourselves against wild boars?"

Heinz laughed. "They won't dare come closer when they see you," he said. "But to be on the safe side, the sentry has this spear as a weapon." He raised a spear over the fire and its steel tip shone.

We nodded agreement.

"Each sentry takes over the spear when he relieves his predecessor according to the rules. For the duration of his watch he won't let the spear out of his hand. If anything happens, he will whistle. If he whistles, everyone will rush out of his tent. Is that clear?"

Otto grunted a tired yes for us all.

"Because there are only a few of us," Heinz continued, "and because standing guard will count as a test of courage, only single sentries will be posted. Each will stand for two hours."

One boy asked, "How will he know the time?"

"Quite right," Heinz agreed. "Who has a watch?"

No one spoke up.

"In that case you'll take mine," he said.

He stood up and took off his wristwatch. "I'll strap it to the flagpole here. Then everybody can see the time whenever he wants to. And the sentries take the responsibility for my watch. Even if it should rain!"

We watched with amusement as Heinz fastened his watch to the pole. His expensive wristwatch!

"Who will volunteer to stand guard this first night?" Heinz asked, looking at each of us in turn. "I'll take the first watch myself."

Günther raised his arm.

I did the same.

Apart from us there were two others who volunteered to stand guard.

Heinz turned down the smallest of the two. Then he asked, "Who'll take the hardest watch, from two to four?"

Günther's arm shot up.

In that way we arrived at the following order. Heinz stood first watch, I relieved him, followed by Günther, followed by the other boy.

We hauled down the flag and sang a song.

Heinz made sure everyone washed.

At ten o'clock precisely Heinz sent us into our tents, reminding the sentries to keep the fire going.

I WAS THERE

I threw three dry branches onto the glowing ashes. Slowly the fire came to life again. With the spear between my knees I moved closer to the fire, dreamily looking into its flames. Slowly I grew warmer.

I came to with a start.

The spear was touching my forehead.

The branches had burned way down.

I was cold. I needed a moment to find myself, then I jumped up and ran to the flagpole.

Half-past one.

To keep myself from falling asleep again, I wandered back and forth among the tents, spear in hand. Twenty-five times I circled the camp before I once more looked at the watch.

It was five minutes before two.

Three more times from pole to last tent and back to the fire. Add more wood. At last it was two o'clock.

Carefully, trying not to wake anyone else, I groped my way through the darkness of the tent to Günther's place: straw, straw—a blanket—a body. It had to be Günther! I shook him.

He turned to the other side, mumbling something.

"Relief's due!" I whispered.

"Oh that!" Günther sat up. "I'm coming."

Quietly I left the tent again. I didn't have to wait long. On all fours Günther crept through the tight opening, stretched, yawned, and rubbed his eyes.

"There's the watch!" I showed it to him. "And here's the spear. Have fun!"

Günther accepted the spear and nodded. "Okay."

I went back into the tent, rolled myself in the blanket and—someone was jerking my leg hard.

"What's up?" I asked, puzzled.

"Come outside!" came a murmur from the entrance.

It took me a long while to wake up properly. Crossly I crawled out of the warm blanket and stumbled out of the tent.

Outside it was dark.

"What time is it?"

Softly Günther answered: "Quarter after two."

I was annoyed. "Why are you dragging me outside again? I just fell asleep!"

"The spear's gone!" Günther said.

"Which spear?"

"The guard spear!"

"Nonsense!" I said. "You took it over from me!"

"Yes!" Günther agreed, "but now it's gone!"

I gradually woke up altogether. But I still didn't understand.

"After you went to lie down, I went to take a piss," Günther explained. "I left the spear stuck in the ground here by the fire. Look, you can still see the hole! When I got back, the spear had disappeared."

"Well, did you notice anything?" I asked. "Or see anyone suspicious?"

Günther shook his head.

"Then the spear can't be gone. At most it's fallen over and rolled away."

Günther disagreed. But we both began to search for it, in ever-larger circles around the fire. Where it was too dark to see, we probed the ground with sticks. With a burning branch lighting our way, we even fanned out beyond the tents. We searched the whole area between the edge of the wood and the stream. We found one rusted flashlight and a knife. No spear! Not even a trace of one!

"We must wake Heinz!"

Günther went to do it.

Drunk with sleep, Heinz staggered out of the tent. At first he wouldn't believe what we told him.

Then we started to search once more.

Heinz even waded into the stream.

No success!

When we gave up, the wristwatch on the pole showed a quarter to four.

"You shouldn't have let the spear out of your hand!" Heinz told Günther. "But there's no point in going on with the search in the dark. Let's lie down. We'll find the spear in the morning when it gets light."

The next morning the fourth sentry complained he hadn't been woken.

Günther had stood guard from two o'clock till six and had searched the whole time. Pale and tired-out, he stood by the fire. When Heinz looked at him, he shrugged his shoulders hopelessly.

Heinz didn't know how to solve the riddle either.

During breakfast Otto turned to Günther and said, "Where's the spear, by the way?"

Dejected, Günther confessed: "Gone!"

Otto grinned. "Bound to happen when you let the spear

out of your hand." He stood up and walked out of the tent. He returned with the spear.

"How did *you* get hold of the spear?" Heinz asked.

"Very simple," said Otto. He pointed to Günther and me. "When they changed over, those two woke me up. I looked out of the tent to ask the time and saw the campground empty. But there was the spear, stuck in the ground by the fire. I took it. Why not, if we have such unreliable sentries?!"

We looked at Otto and said nothing.

He was completely unaffected by our looks. He went on chewing.

Casually he said, "Incidentally, that's a guard violation. And guard violations are supposed to be punished particularly severely."

Heinz ignored the remark.

Nobody took it up.

"Favoritism!" grumbled Otto.

"I'm sorry, Günther," Heinz said then. "Otto is right. You should neither have left your post nor allowed the spear out of your hand. You'll have to accept suitable punishment." He turned to us. "Any suggestions as to the kind of punishment Günther should receive?"

With a side glance at Günther, Otto said, "Send him home! He's not a real man!"

Crushed, his head bowed, Günther accepted our judgment. Everyone turned down Otto's proposal, and most spoke up for Günther. It almost turned into a fight because we couldn't agree on a punishment.

Finally Heinz intervened. "Enough!" he said. "Because

Günther lost the spear while on duty, he will guard the camp this morning while the rest of us go on a hike. Agreed?"

Everyone agreed. Except Otto, who protested: "So he can catch up on his sleep? Can't even look after one spear!" But no one listened to him.

"Will you accept the punishment, Günther?" Heinz asked.

Günther looked at the ground and nodded.

The Oberjungstammführer

The sky was a uniform gray. It had been drizzling for the last half-hour. Small puddles were beginning to form, and the ground was sodden beneath our feet.

Our uniforms soaked up the rain. We were chilly. Together with two other *Fähnleins,* we stood in an open square and listened to the speech of our *Oberjungstammführer.*

Our region's youth leader talked and talked and talked. He spoke of the Führer, the ordinary corporal of World War I, of the German armed forces and the work of the Führer. He spoke about us members of the *Jungvolk* and our duty to mature into first-class soldiers.

We had stopped listening. The boys in the first rank

were absent-mindedly staring at the overcast sky. In the ranks toward the rear, boys were playing with their fingers or cleaning out their pockets. The restiveness spread through the audience.

The *Oberjungstammführer* seemed to feel the growing discomfort. His eyes wandered from right to left; he was trying to discover who was causing the disturbance.

"You know," Günther whispered, nudging Heinz in his side, "he wants to turn us all into soldiers."

Heinz nodded.

The speaker had stopped speaking.

No one moved. Everyone was alert, looked across to our corner if they could. All were waiting.

"Who spoke just now?" snarled the youth leader.

Silence.

Günther and Heinz pretended to look around, then looked innocently at the official. Those of us sitting next to them tried to look as unconcerned as possible.

"Who was it who talked?" the voice asked again. The leader was approaching our platoon.

Those who were uninvolved followed what was happening as if it was a play.

We were beginning to feel more uncomfortable.

The *Oberjungstammführer* turned red. "This platoon only," he said, pointing at us. "At attention!"

Our heels cracked together as one. All tried to stand perfectly: hands pressed flat against trouser seams, elbows angled slightly forward, chests out, heads straight, eyes fixed. We suspected everything mattered now.

"I want to know which of you has been babbling?" the party official demanded. "Step forward, whoever it is!"

The platoon stood motionless; not a single eyelid twitched.

"I will count until three and the blabbermouth will speak up! One—two—three! Well? So you don't want to? Platoon leader!"

With five firm steps Heinz had stepped to the front. In perfect form, he stopped in front of the official.

"Who in your unit has blabbed?"

Heinz stood even straighter. "I do not know, sir. I heard nothing!"

His superior's neck began to swell. His head turned even redder. He gestured wildly. "What? You cover for the dirty swine in your platoon! And you want to be a leader!" His voice broke. "You are nothing, nothing at all!" he screeched. "I will—"

"I was the one who spoke, sir!" said Günther, lifting his arm.

The *Oberjungstammführer* broke off, disconcerted. He looked at Heinz and Günther in turn. "We will talk later!" he shouted at Heinz. "Fall into line!"

Heinz walked, pale and serious, back to his position.

All at once the leader's voice turned very soft. Smiling kindly, he said to Günther, "Step forward!" Günther pushed his way out of the ranks backward, ran around the unit, and positioned himself three steps in front of the *Oberjungstammführer*.

"So it was you, eh?" said the leader in a near-whisper.

We were straining to hear every word, no longer felt the cold and the dampness.

"What did you say?" the official asked Günther.

Günther said nothing.

The official moved closer to him. "What did you say?"

Günther pressed his lips together.

"Answer!" roared the *Oberjungstammführer* in a voice so loud we recoiled in fear.

But Günther did not answer.

Resolutely the leader turned around. Facing us all, he declared: "I will now give you a taste of how the German *Wehrmacht* handles such deceitful and obstinate people, how they make them break." He raised his voice. "The following orders are meant only for this one!" he said, pointing at Günther.

"Lie down!"

Günther threw himself to the ground.

"Up! Quick-march!"

Günther picked himself up and ran forward.

In front of a large puddle: "Lie down!"

Günther let himself fall beside the puddle.

"What? You refuse to execute orders? Up!" Günther leaped up. His pants and tunic showed muddy patches.

"Two steps to the right!"

Günther followed the order. Now he stood exactly in front of the puddle.

"Down!"

The water splashed high.

"Slide!"

Günther pushed himself on his stomach through the slimy water.

"Turn about!"

In the middle of the puddle, at its deepest spot, Günther turned around and, still on his stomach, slid to the edge.

"Up! Quick-march!"

Dripping, soiled from face to shoes, Günther ran through the square. Mud flew from his clothes as he ran.

"Attention!"

Facing the *Oberjungstammführer,* Günther stood to attention.

"Knees, bend!"

Arms held out in front of him, Günther sank into the crouch.

"Hop!"

In the crouch, Günther hopped across the empty square. When he splashed through puddles, the water sprayed his face. A dark liquid dribbled from his hair. He was swaying as he moved.

"Attention!"

Again Günther pulled himself upright.

"About face!"

Günther turned to face us.

"Look at the dirty pig!" jeered the *Oberjungstamm-führer.*

"Take cover!"

Without looking around, Günther dropped down and pressed his face into the sludgy ground.

"Attention!"

Günther got up.

The *Oberjungstammführer* was grinning. "Five steps forward!"

Günther obeyed. The last step brought him once more to the edge of the large puddle.

"I must spare my voice. You will observe my thumb signs and follow them. This means 'Lie down!' " With closed fist the official pointed his stretched-out thumb downward. "And this means 'Up!' " He pointed toward the sky. "Let's go!"

The thumb pointed down. Günther flung himself into the water.

The thumb was raised. Günther shot up.

Thumb down.

The water spurted high.

Thumb up.

The water streamed back into the puddle.

Down!

Up!

Down!

Up!

And we watched at attention.

VI

-1938-

The Fathers

"The schnitzel was excellent," my father said, and leaned back.

Mother smiled gratefully. She got up, gathered the plates, and carried them out to the kitchen.

"And you?" Father turned to me. "Already in uniform again? What's on today? Where are you off to?"

"I have a date with Heinz and Günther," I replied. "We want to prepare our *Heim* celebration in honor of the Führer's birthday."

"That's right," Father recalled. "Next week Adolf has another birthday. He'll be forty-nine. That'll be some celebration, I bet! And just wait till next year when he'll be fifty. Then they'll fall all over themselves with songs and rejoicing."

Mother came back to the living room to remove the tablecloth.

"Well, Mother, what'll you set before us on the Führer's birthday?" Father asked, laughing.

Mother didn't have to think long. *"Eintopf!"* she said, "because it'll be the first Sunday of the month and you know we're supposed to have stew once a month!"

"But Mother," Father remonstrated, "he really deserves better than that. You'll have to admit he has accomplished quite a bit. Do you remember how we lived before 1933? We didn't have any veal cutlets then! And I was out of work and my unemployment benefits barely covered the rent. We didn't have enough to eat. We suffered hunger, real hunger. It's hard to imagine that today. We had no clothes, our furniture was taken to the pawnbroker's piece after piece, and I either hung around the employment office or sat on a park bench somewhere to get away from the worry in your face, Mother. If Grandfather hadn't helped us then...!"

Mother nodded. "We are better off today," she agreed, "but on the other hand, others are doing worse. Think of the Jews! And Günther's father."

"Well," Father said, "Hitler has this spleen about Jews. But then everyone is a bit crazy somewhere. He'll calm down, you'll see. It has already grown much quieter; it looked much worse in the beginning. I am ashamed I tried to talk the Schneiders into emigrating back in those days."

"Who knows, who knows?" Mother shook her head. "Perhaps it would have been better if they had gone."

"Let it be, Mother. It's in the past. At least we are better off. I have work again, I earn enough, and we have enough to eat. Sometimes we can treat ourselves to a bottle of wine. We are dressed cleanly and neatly; we have new furniture in our apartment, and every four weeks we go to a movie or to the theater."

"And above all," Mother added, "we no longer have to accept handouts from Grandfather. No longer can he tell us we've failed!"

Father grew more expansive. "Soon we may even be able to afford a trip to the Norwegian fjords with *Kraft durch Freude*. And as soon as I have enough stamps on my savings card, we will drive along the Autobahns in our own Volkswagen. Then we'll get to know all of Germany, the *Ostmark,* and who knows what else." Father beamed. "And whom can we thank for it all?"

Mother smiled.

Father's eyes sparkled with enthusiasm. "Go on, boy! Off with you! And put together a worthy celebration!"

"You want the young gentleman." The maid in the black dress with the little bonnet and small white apron smiled. She asked me to come in and led me to the large room with drapes the same color red as our flag. "He'll be a while yet," she explained. "They're still at the table."

When she had left the room, I threw myself into one of the soft armchairs. A moment later Heinz appeared. He only came as far as the doorway. "We're still eating!" he called. "But we'll be finished soon." He pushed one of the double doors all the way open and went off again.

In rolled a little tea wagon with a glass of tea, a bowl of sugar, and a tiny milk jug. "Madam sends you this," the maid informed me, and quietly withdrew.

I was still playing with the sugar tongs when Heinz and his father came in.

"I have something special for you two," Heinz's father said. "Wait a second!" He crossed the large room and went into the room next door.

We looked after him expectantly. We saw him take something from a closet.

It was an almost life-sized portrait of Adolf Hitler, framed behind glass. "I'll make you a present of it."

We didn't know what to say. We even forgot to say thank you.

"Well, is it a surprise?"

Heinz put his arm around my shoulder. "It certainly is!" he said.

His father was pleased. "I thought you could use it in your *Heim*."

Heinz thought. "We'll unveil it on the Führer's birthday, Father."

His father agreed. "That's a good idea," he said. "You can arrange a suitable ceremony and at its height you un-veil the picture. In a short address you can point out that the Führer has been sent to us by God, that he would never have been able to clear up the German mess so quickly and thoroughly otherwise. Who would have thought, five years ago, that a simple corporal would lead Germany to such greatness? This man is not obsessed by ambition like so many before him. What does he get out of life? He doesn't smoke, he doesn't drink, he eats no meat, he even does without a family. All that remains is work, work and worry about us. Think of it, boys. All of us should try to become as selfless as our Führer. Without that selflessness he would never have been able to create a Greater Germany in the space of five years.

"For the first time in German history, Germans are sticking together and unanimously proclaiming their loyalty to one man, to our Führer Adolf Hitler. And boys, we are only at the beginning of the path Hitler wants to lead us along. He will require a great deal from us still, but we can also expect a lot from him. Germany will grow larger, will become more beautiful if only we will give our whole strength to the Führer so he will be able to realize his great plans. The Führer will not only help us Germans to power and respect, he will also reorganize the world. Boys, I envy you the future you will be privileged to experience. Everything that today costs us effort and difficulties will come true for you and your children." His eyes had suddenly begun to shine. Softly he said: "Honestly, boys, I am happy to be a German at this moment in time."

We remained silent.

Heinz was the first to break the quiet. "Thank you very much, Father, for the picture."

Heinz's father waved away his thanks. "Don't mention it," he said. "Enjoy it! And now away with you!"

The Fathers

"Sit down!" Günther's father invited us. "Günther's out getting soup from the butcher. He should be back soon."

Günther's mother pushed chairs toward us.

On the table stood three soup plates, each of which had a different pattern. One had a piece missing from the rim. Günther's father sat before a plate decorated with garlands of flowers. His hands were playing with a spoon. He was looking at us thoughtfully.

I avoided his eyes and looked at the three cups without handles on the wall shelf above the stove.

Günther's mother was working by the kitchen cabinet.

Finally Günther appeared. He nodded to us. "It's only leftovers," he explained as he handed the pot to his mother. "That's all the butcher had left. We should come earlier in the future, he said."

His mother lifted the lid and looked into the pot. Then she tipped the contents into two plates. The third, the broken one with the onion pattern, she returned to the cabinet.

She took a loaf of black bread from the breadbox. She cut off three slices, each the thickness of a thumb. With her slice she sat down at the place without a plate. She broke the bread and dipped it into her husband's soup.

Again Günther's father looked at me. From me his look strayed to Heinz, then slid across to his son. At last he asked, "What are your plans?"

Günther peered unobtrusively at me and continued to spoon up his soup without replying.

"We want to get the *Heim* ready," I explained readily, "so that. . . ."

Günther cleared his throat.

I fell silent.

Quietly, a little sadly, Günther's father said: "What have you turned my son into, you and your *Jungvolk* and your Führer?" He sat back in his chair, leaving the spoon in the soup and pushing the plate toward his wife.

"Let it be, Father," Günther's mother said as she soothingly placed her hand on his fist. "We have to reconcile ourselves to the times at some point."

"Reconcile, reconcile!" her husband protested. "Can you reconcile yourself to the fact that our whole family has been destroyed in a few years?" He stood up and paced back and forth in the kitchen. "And I stand here, hands in my pockets, and let it happen. My boy screams 'Sieg Heil! Sieg Heil!' and lets himself be dragged along by that brown swine, while his mother works herself to death because his father can't. His father's an ex-convict who doesn't even dare to speak out! A man turned into a convict by Hitler!"

Günther lowered his head over his plate. His ears had turned red.

Heinz stared fixedly at nothing.

Günther's father bent down to his wife. He spoke emphatically to her. "The boys all let themselves be intoxicated by his successes. They don't even notice that this stupid man is leading them to disaster. It just can't turn out well: Hitler creates the *Wehrmacht;* Hitler occupies the Rhineland; Hitler rearms the country; Hitler names himself 'Supreme Commander of the *Wehrmacht*'; Hitler 'takes' Austria 'back into the Reich!' Next perhaps he'll take the Sudetenland, Upper Silesia, and West Prussia, then the Memel district, Northern Schleswig, Eupen-et-Mal-médy, Alsace-Lorraine, and finally the colonies and the whole world. Where will it end? I ask you, Mother, where will it end? Do you seriously think the whole world will tolerate this forever? Hitler brings us war! War, Mother!"

Günther's mother clasped her husband's wrists. "Do be quiet! Think of the boys!"

Breathing deeply, the father talked on. "Who will tell the boys if I am quiet, Mother? They must know this after all! They must know that Hitler will bring them misfortune instead of salvation."

"Father!" shouted Günther's mother. "Stop! Won't you ever learn!"

Günther's father smiled a pained smile. "Cautious? Cautious until death! You always want to learn to be cautious, but you rush into ruin with your caution. Let them put me behind bars again! Let them! I can't watch them march, singing, to their ruin, my Günther carrying the flag at their head. . . ."

He pounded the table with both fists. He looked as if he was about to cry.

"Leave!"

Heinz was already by the door.

Günther's mother pushed her son and me out of the kitchen. "Please, boys, go and forget what you have heard," she begged.

Raw Materials

"We three go together," decided Heinz, "and we'll see if we can't collect more than the others."

Günther shouldered one of the empty sacks. "Where do we begin?" he asked.

"We'd best begin with a house with the number one," I suggested. "We'll stay on that side of the street until we get to the last house. Then we'll turn around and go in the opposite direction on the other side of the street back to the start. And we'll ring the bells on every floor."

The two smiled at me.

"You're a clever child." Heinz hit me on the shoulder and handed me an empty sack. Try it your way. We'll watch."

They took me to a two-family house. "Start here!" they urged. "We'll wait." They sat down on a garden wall opposite the house.

I felt uncomfortable, but I had to prove what my suggestion was worth. Heinz and Günther, empty sacks on their knees, grinned after me.

I rang the bell and waited.

Nothing.

I rang again.

Again nothing. But, yes! The curtain was moving at a window on the street floor.

I waited.

No one opened the door.

I stood outside the door for a long time.

"Go to the next house!" shouted the two from their wall. "Otherwise we'll lose too much time!"

I took their advice. The next house resembled the first. Three bells, one above the other. You could see the people living here were well off.

I pushed the bottom bell.

Steps approached the door. A man opened.

"Heil Hitler!" I greeted him. "I—"

"I am Jewish!" the man barked and slammed the door.

The next house had at least five floors.

"Why don't you go from top to bottom," suggested the two on the wall. "Otherwise you won't even get into the houses."

I pressed the top bell.

A buzzer opened the door.

The sack wedged beneath my arm, I climbed six flights of stairs and reached the top out of breath.

At the door beside the entrance to the attic stood a very young woman with a baby. The baby was screaming.

"You woke him up!" the woman said.

"Heil Hitler!" I brought out with an effort. I tried to explain what I wanted, but the louder I spoke, the louder the baby screamed.

The woman finally managed to quiet the child.

"I've come to ask if you have any old things to spare for the public collection," I blurted out.

The young woman smiled. "Where would I get old things, boy? We have hardly anything new. I can't even offer you old paper. I use the paper from the previous day to light our stove in the morning."

Speechless and disappointed, I leaned against the banister. I couldn't think of what to do next.

"Why don't you try the second floor?" the young woman was saying. "The owner lives there. He'll be more likely to have something for you."

I thanked her and apologized and thanked her again and walked down the stairs. Very hesitantly I rang the owner's bell.

A man with glasses looked through the mailbox flap in the door.

"What do you want?" he asked.

I repeated my little speech.

"So, scrap iron and old paper, eh?" He cleared his throat. "You must be at least the tenth to come asking for it. Last month they sawed off the iron fence in my front yard. Boy, if I had as much scrap iron as you want, I'd start a business myself. Let the Führer see where he gets the cannons to shoot the Czechs. I can't supply him any. I am sorry. I prefer to eat butter!" And he let the flap fall closed.

"Well, how much did you get?" the two on the wall wanted to know. I pointed to my empty sack.

"It doesn't work my way," I admitted meekly.

"How many times have you tried it before?" Heinz asked.

"Never!"

"It's no good anyway," Heinz decided. "D'you know what would happen if we followed your suggestion? We'd end up sitting on the curb somewhere, at number 37 or such, the bottom of the sack barely covered. But we wouldn't be able to walk another step and we'd have to drag ourselves up by the banisters when we got home."

Günther laughed. "Wait and see! We'll do something quite different. Come on!"

We walked toward the town center.

"First to the hardware store?" Günther asked Heinz at the main street. He pointed to a gloomy store across the street.

"No!" Heinz said "Everyone goes there first." He looked around "Let's try the stationery store."

"Scrap iron at a stationery store?" I asked in amazement.

Heinz nodded. "That's *why!* And you, keep back a bit."

We entered the store. We positioned ourselves side by side in front of the woman at the cash register and saluted.

"How very nice that you're coming to me, too!" the woman said delightedly. "I still have a few things in the cellar." She turned the cash register over to a clerk and motioned us to follow her.

In the cellar lay whole mountains of old pencil boxes, rusty pencil sharpeners, dented piggy banks, and unusable souvenirs—all made from either tin or iron.

We eagerly threw everything into our sacks.

"Don't strain your backs!" the woman warned.

We filled one sack to the top, the other halfway.

"Unfortunately I don't have any scrap paper," the woman said with regret in her voice. "I always have it pulped."

Heinz solemnly assured her we were well satisfied even so. Then he lifted the sacks onto Günther's back and mine, thanked the woman in all our names, and promised to come back at the next opportunity.

Back upstairs, the woman gave each of us a new crayon.

"We have enough for today," Günther said contentedly.

We hauled the sacks to the nearest streetcar stop and rested on one of the benches. Heinz opened the heavy sack. On top lay lots of metal casings for matchboxes. All were stamped with Hitler's picture. Many were badly rusted.

Heinz selected the three in the best condition. "If we polish them up," he suggested, "we'll have beautiful keepsakes."

Crystal Night

"You took part?" asked Heinz.

"Yes!" I admitted.

"Where?"

"At the home for apprentices—but only for a short time."

"Why?"

"I don't know," I confessed. "At first I only looked on, and suddenly I was right in the middle of it all. I don't know how it happened."

Heinz sighed. "One could weep over you! Weren't you once friends with the boy who lives above you?"

I nodded.

"And then you go and smash those people's things to bits."

"I didn't do that!" I remonstrated.

"But you were there!" Heinz accused me.

"I took part, too," Günther declared.

Heinz froze. "You, too?"

Günther raised his shoulders. "I had to," he said.

"What do you mean, 'had to'?" Heinz bristled. "No one *had* to!"

"I did. They made me!" Günther replied.

"Who made you do something against Jews?" Heinz demanded. "You weren't even allowed to!"

"What?"

Heinz hesitated a moment, then looked at his feet. "It had been ordered that the Hitler Youth and the *Jungvolk* were not to participate," he said in a quiet voice.

"Ordered?"

"Yes, ordered," Heinz confirmed.

"I thought it all happened spontaneously—people's rage or something!?" Günther said, sounding surprised.

"Nonsense!"

"But that's what Goebbels claims!" Günther remembered.

"Nonsense I said!" In a barely audible voice, Heinz told us: "I accidentally listened in to a long-distance telephone conversation my father had about it."

"Afterward?" Günther inquired.

Heinz shook his head. "Before! My father had to put together the list of Jewish apartments and businesses."

I WAS THERE

Günther stepped close to Heinz. "And you didn't warn us." He turned away. "And you call yourself a friend?"

Heinz looked up. "Should I have dragged my father into it?"

Some time later Günther told his story, jerkily and in a harsh voice:

"I'm coming out of school. I need a new math notebook, so I walk over to Abraham Rosenthal's store. I climb down the stairs to his tiny cellar store.

"The door's locked. I knock. Nothing. I knock harder. And the old man with the goatee looks out at me from behind a shelf unit.

"I wave to him.

"He recognizes me, very carefully glides through the store, and opens up. 'What do you want?' he asks.

" 'I'd like a math notebook,' I say.

"He shakes his head. 'Go home,' he says, and tries to close the door.

"I push my foot in between. 'What's the matter? I need that notebook.'

"So he leaves the door open. I step inside, close the door, and follow him into the store.

"He takes down one of the fat notebooks with a stiff cover. I say, 'No, I don't have enough money for that. Give me a thin one.'

"But he hands me the notebook and tries to push me out of the store. 'I'll give it to you!' he says. 'Go on home!'

"I think the old man's gone crazy. I take the money from my pocket and put it on the table.

"At that moment they arrive. They are yelling and screaming. The old man flees behind his shelves.

"The door is flung open. It smashes against the wall, shattering the glass window.

"I turn around.

"Someone rips the notebook out of my hand and hits me in the face with it. 'You pig, buying from Jews!' he shouts.

"The little store is suddenly full of people. Someone is pulling the old man back and forth by his goatee. He pushes him against a shelf so hard that everything on it falls off.

"The man who hit me pushes a large jar of chocolates into my hand. I stand there, holding the jar.

" 'Throw it!' he commands.

"But I can't do it.

"The old man is standing right opposite me, and he's looking at me. They've pressed his arms against the shelf as if they were crucifying him.

" 'Throw the jar in front of his feet!' The man ordered again.

"I hold the jar tightly.

"He comes to stand behind me. 'I'll count till three. One —' It has become utterly quiet in the store. Everyone's watching.

" 'Two—'

"They are pressing in closer, leaving only the space between the old man and me clear.

" 'Three!'

I WAS THERE

"I am still clutching the jar.

"The man kicks me in the rear. 'Will you get on with it, you pig!' he screams.

"The old man with the goatee nods to me.

"And I throw the jar at his feet.

"The splinters jump as high as my knees. The candy flies through the store. Everyone starts to cheer, to pull paper and candy off the shelves. They trample it. They smash ink bottles and dye the man's goatee blue with the ink. They tear notebooks to shreds, thick ones and thin ones.

"The man from before hits me in the neck. 'Get out!' he snaps.

"But I can't leave. Curious onlookers stand pressed close together on the stairs to the cellar, watching.

"I see someone punch the old man in the stomach, see the Jew collapse.

"They drag him out of the store, up the stairs, away.

"Most of them run after him.

"I bend down for my notebook, but I can't find it.

"A few have stayed behind and throw the paper and the rest of the junk onto the street. I go home."

VII
-1939-

In the Hitler Youth

I was polishing my Hitler Youth dagger. The words "Blood and Honor" etched into it showed up clearly. I had even polished the Hitler Youth mark stamped onto the black handle till it shone.

The others were talking in low voices.

Günther sat in the seat next to Heinz. He was tugging at his new red-white-red armband. On his sleeve below the armband you could still make out a lighter spot, where the Jungvolk's rune of victory used to be.

"You should fasten it with three stitches," Heinz recommended. "Otherwise it'll keep slipping down, or the swastika will turn to the inside."

Günther nodded. "My mother can do that. She still

has to sew the buttons on my shoulder straps as well."

Curious, Heinz pulled at Günther's shoulder straps. "How did you fasten them?" he asked.

"With safety pins."

The door opened.

We looked up and stopped talking.

A gorgeous fragrance wafted into the room. We sniffed it with astonishment.

A blond platoon leader in Hitler Youth uniform minced in behind it. Cologne filled the room to the last corner.

There wasn't a hair out of place, or a speck of dust on his uniform. His shoes were polished to a hard shine. He walked up and held out his hand to Heinz, a hand as fine as a girl's, and in a curiously soft voice he said: "You and your *Jungvolk* platoon have joined the Hitler Youth as a whole. I am pleased to make your acquaintance. We need good leaders in the Hitler Youth."

Heinz said nothing.

A smile on his face, the sweet-smelling platoon leader looked us over. "Nice boys you brought," he remarked as he walked along the front row. He stroked everyone's hair and repeated, "Really—nice boys." When he came to Otto, he chucked him under the chin and raised his head, forced him to meet his gaze.

"We will be friends," he said in a velvety voice. Then he pirouetted around on the tips of his toes.

We sat silently. We looked at each other.

The door opened again.

This time it was our new *Gefolgschaftsführer* who had finally arrived.

In the Hitler Youth

"Attention!"

We leaped up from our seats.

The fragrant platoon leader reported.

His superior honored Heinz with neither a greeting nor a glance. He thanked the reporting Hitler Youth platoon leader and ordered us to sit down.

Our eyes wandered from one leader to the other. We waited. The *Gefolgschaftsführer* cleared his throat. "Quite a lot will change for you in the Hitler Youth," he began without greeting. "First, you are no longer *Pimpfs,* but Hitler Youths: you bear the name of our Führer. Second, this obliges you even more than before to demonstrate always and everywhere why the Führer has chosen you. All childish behavior stops forthwith. Third, I regard it as the mission of the Hitler Youth to prepare you for your upcoming military service. With the recovery of the Ostmark, the Sudetenland, and the Memel district, and the dissolution of Czechoslovakia, the creation of a Greater German Reich and a reordering of Europe are no longer out of our reach. Fourth, in order that we may fulfill the mission given us, we need experienced leaders. Only trial in service will prove whether former leaders among you can be utilized further. Fifth, the Hitler Youth, consisting as it does of young working men, apprentices, and school boys, requires different hours. Duty in the Hitler Youth, therefore, falls primarily on evenings and Sundays. Sixth, Sundays belong to the Hitler Youth, not to going to church. You are old enough now to discard bourgeois prejudices. Seventh, I expect absolute loyalty to the Führer. The enemies of the Führer are your enemies, too, be they Jews,

Bolsheviks, parsons, or whatever. Eighth, I demand from you unwavering dedication to the ideals of National Socialism. The Führer's word is both command and revelation. Ninth, I demand from you the readiness to sacrifice blood and life for Führer, Folk, and Fatherland. To be a Hitler Youth is to be a hero. Tenth, hundredth, and thousandth: I demand obedience, obedience, unconditional obedience."

I was expecting more. But the recital had ended.

"Up!" shouted the *Gefolgschaftsführer*. "And now our song 'Forward':

> "Forward! Forward! with resounding fanfares,
> Forward! Forward! Youth knows no peril.
> Germany, you will stand resplendent
> although we may die.
> Forward! Forward! with resounding fanfares.
> Forward! Forward! Youth knows no peril.
> Be the goal ever so high,
> youth will gain it.
> Our banner precedes us, fluttering in the breeze,
> as we march into the future, man after man.
> We'll march for Hitler through night and
>   through danger
> with the flag of youth, for freedom and bread.
> Our banner precedes us, fluttering in the breeze.
> Our banner signals the new time.
> Our banner leads us to eternity.
> Yes, our banner is worth more than death."

Our first Hitler Youth meeting was over. On the way home I said, "I don't like it in the Hitler Youth."

"I don't either," Günther promptly agreed. "I don't either."

Heinz walked between us, looking thoughtful. He was staring ahead as fixedly as he had in the kitchen with Günther's father. After a long while he said softly, without looking at us: "We will have to get used to it."

Hiking

The packs weighed heavy. For two hours we had been trudging uphill and downhill, in between hedges and around farms, and all in darkness.

"Surely there never used to be this many fences and barriers," grumbled Heinz.

"We've lost our way," Otto whimpered.

"No!" Heinz declared. "This is the right path, you can be sure of that! We'll be getting there soon."

Grumbling to ourselves, we shuffled on.

"Who was it who picked that idiot train that traveled half the night?" someone said.

"I!" said Heinz. "Nothing wrong with the train. According to the timetable it should have arrived around five o'clock. It's not *my* fault it had to let twenty others go by."

"Yes!" fumed Günther, "and nothing but freight trains,

too. And every single one was loaded with cement and iron bars. Is cement more important than we are I ask you?"

No one answered.

We were stumbling up a stony path. Everything was pitch dark. Not a star anywhere.

"Damn!" muttered Otto. "Those farmers ruin every path with their damn tractors."

"I can't understand it," Heinz said. "Last year there was nothing here but farm wagons." He let his flashlight flare up briefly. "But these tracks weren't made by farm wagons."

Silently we followed one another. There was no sound apart from breathing.

"I'm tired," a boy complained.

"Not long now," Heinz consoled him.

Suddenly our marching column came to a halt.

"This is the spot," Heinz announced from the head of the column. He flung his pack to the ground.

Otto looked around. "A beautiful view!" he jeered.

"Quick! Put up the tents and go to sleep!" Heinz said.

"And where do we get the straw?" someone asked.

"Nowhere," Günther replied. "We'll dispense with straw for tonight. It's not cold. If we roll ourselves into our blankets we'll manage fine. We'll get straw tomorrow. All I want to do right now is sleep."

Heinz shone his light along the ground. "What a mess!" He swore. "The farmers have obviously been spreading fertilizer here. This white muck's everywhere. But I won't go any farther now! The spot here is fairly clean." He put his flashlight on the ground at such an angle that we could all work in its light. "You, Günther, and I, we'll build a three-man tent," he told me. "Give me your tarpaulin."

I fumbled through my things in the dark.

The others were sorting out poles and buttoning tarpaulins together.

Otto was grumbling as he hammered the first pegs into the earth.

"Do we have to dig trenches?" a voice asked out of the darkness.

"Pray that it won't rain," Günther replied. "Everything else we'll do tomorrow."

"Which ass has buttoned my jacket into the tarpaulin?" someone ranted.

"Ass yourself!" was the answer.

Otherwise everything was quiet. Occasionally there was a suppressed swearword, a muffled thud, a ping of steel on steel.

"Our tent's up!" Otto reported.

"Good! Go and lie down!" Heinz ordered.

"And who's on guard duty?" said Otto.

"If you all agree," Heinz suggested, "we'll dispense with it for once. In the darkness no one'll rob us, and we'll simply take our things into the tents with us."

No one disagreed. One after the other we crept into our tents. Heinz was the last. He brought the flashlight with him. Günther was already asleep.

Our whole tent shook.

I woke up.

"Did you ram the pegs in properly?" Günther asked me, still half asleep. "A cow's obviously paying us a visit."

Through the gap at the entrance an enormous, very bald head was looking in.

"The moon in person!" Günther said.

"Hey! Sleepyheads!" rumbled the bald head. "How did you get here?"

Sleepily, Heinz peered out of his blanket. "If you must know the exact details, we landed yesterday on board the *Bremen*."

The bald man didn't seem to feel like joking. "Don't get fresh with me!" he said. "You can't stay here!"

"Why not?" Günther asked.

"Because it's prohibited, that's why!" the man thundered back.

"Who prohibited it?" said Günther.

"The Führer, that's who!" shouted the bald man. "The Supreme Commander of the *Wehrmacht!*"

"I didn't know the Führer owned a plot of land here," Günther said with a yawn and lay down again.

The bald man went into a rage.

The tent threatened to collapse.

"But I used to be able to camp here before!" Heinz put in.

The man laughed an artificial laugh. "Used to—but no more! Times have changed. Come on, out with you! Pack up your junk and take it somewhere else! And get a move on!" His head disappeared from the opening.

"The guy's soft in the head!" Heinz whispered. "I've

been coming here for three years. The land belongs to the state and the forester's always given permission—I know him well. But this bald head is new. I never saw *him* before—"

We heard a commotion outside.

A moment later the tousled head of Otto appeared at the tent entrance. "You sure led us to a beautiful part of the country," he sneered. "Really stunning!"

Aimed perfectly, Günther's drinking mug sailed through the gap. But Otto was no longer there.

We scrambled out of our blankets.

Günther was the first to put his head outside. He pulled it in again at once. He looked at us in horror. "Where have we landed?"

We kicked off our blankets and crept out of the tent as fast as we could.

A surprise awaited us. We were camped on the single green spot in a vast building site. Stacks of wooden boards, tool sheds, storage houses full of sacks of cement and hundreds of steel railings surrounded us.

"But none of this was here last year," Heinz burst out.

The bald head was standing among our tents, hands planted firmly on his hips. "Last year," he replied, "last year we weren't building the Siegfried Line (Westwall) either."

Our sheepish faces made him more conciliatory. "I still don't understand how you found the way here. Come with me. Just look!"

Unwashed, uncombed, covered with cement dust, we

hesitantly followed. The path was much wider than one made by truck tracks. On both sides embankments dropped off steeply into five- or six-meter-deep pits. The ground in some of these had already been surfaced with reinforced concrete. A high board fence enclosed the gigantic building site. Only the entrance was open. At the entrance stood a small guard house. Propped against it was a sign that read: FORBIDDEN ZONE! KEEP OUT!

"But why didn't the guard stop us?" Heinz asked.

The bald head scratched his pate. "Well, I guess I must've dozed off for a while."

We laughed.

And he joined in.

As we dismantled the tents, Günther said: "At least I now know why the cement trains were in such a hurry."

It was getting dark.

The others were already asleep in their tents.

Heinz, Günther, and I were sitting by the campfire.

Heinz was poking around in the ashes. "I find this spot better than the one below," he remarked.

"You can see farther!" I agreed.

"Yes," Günther said. "I can see seven building sites from here. Eight if I stand up."

We said nothing.

The first stars appeared in the dark blue sky. I unbuckled my hiking shoes.

Heinz had thrown his stick away and was staring aimlessly into the distance when Günther suddenly began, "I don't like all this. To be honest I've never liked it, not ever. Not in the *Jungvolk* and not in the Hitler Youth, especially not in the Hitler Youth." He stopped.

Heinz looked at him inquiringly. Calmly he pulled up his legs and waited.

After a while Günther continued. "I'd never have come to you on my own! I joined because I had to; you forced me to do it. I found it hard once I'd come. Everything you talked about and thought seemed both distant and strange to me. I never felt at one with you." He picked up a partially charred stick and very slowly drew a swastika in the earth. He surrounded it with a large circle. Then he quickly scratched out both.

Heinz and I kept quiet.

It took a long time before Günther spoke again, and what he said didn't seem meant for us. It sounded as if he was merely trying to understand himself.

"Yes, I chatted along with you, I joined in. Sometimes, rarely—very rarely—it was even really beautiful! For an hour, a whole afternoon at a time, I'd be happy. But mostly I found it hell, felt like spitting at you. But then I'd always think of my father." He shook himself.

Heinz wrapped his arms around his legs. I cautiously stretched my feet toward the ashes. It had turned completely dark.

Günther whipped his stick up and down. "And I don't even know what it is that makes you seem so strange to me. I've thought about it, but I don't know. You are different—so cold somehow. You talk, plan, confer. You are so sure about everything. I don't understand you. All I know is that I don't belong with you."

Heinz had propped his chin on his knees and was staring straight ahead when Günther turned to look at him. "I participated only because of you, Heinz. You were a decent guy. You were older, brighter, capable. I had always admired you. I wanted to have you for a friend. In you I believed. What Heinz did couldn't be wrong."

Heinz didn't move.

Günther looked away from him.

I didn't dare move.

The fire had gone out altogether.

It was a moonless, dark night. Only the stars flickered far away, uninvolved.

A bird's cry tore the stillness.

"I think my father's always been right. You only seek power! You're driving us into war!" And in almost a wail: "But you, Heinz, you!?" Günther leaped up. From his trouser pocket he took the matchbox cover with the Führer's picture on it. He removed the box, crumpled the casing, and threw the remains down the slope.

Only then did Heinz raise his head. "I, yes, I! But what can I do?"

Plans

We sat cross-legged on the table.

Heinz was saying calmly, "The Poles provoked us for so long we couldn't do anything else. We had to show them that you can't deny the Greater German Reich its rights. Within eighteen days Poland was conquered. Sure, the French and the English felt obliged to declare war on us while we were advancing into Poland. They were bound by treaty to do that. But now Poland doesn't exist any more—we've occupied one half, Russia the other. Tell me what would tie England and France to a country that no longer exists? The Führer has made them a generous peace proposal. Why aren't they accepting the offered hand?" He stopped to look at each of us. "I'll tell you why. They don't want peace, they want war! We have no alternative but to march against them too and defeat them. And all Germans must stand together in his war. As soon as I am seventeen, I'll volunteer—"

"By the time we're old enough," Otto interrupted him, "the war will be over. And I'd so like to join our air force."

In vain, Heinz tried to continue. Otto went right on, "The pilots get better rations, and they also have the smartest uniforms. What'll you think when I swoop down on London in my Stuka bomber and—" He interrupted the gesture imitating the dive and looked at us, at a loss. "What's important to destroy in London?"

"Westminster Abbey!"

"No, the docks!"

"Both are fine by me!" Otto decided. "First Westminster, and at the second approach the docks. The Tommies'll have the pieces flying around their ears."

War fever had suddenly gripped us all. Heinz couldn't get a word in edgewise.

"But that's ridiculous!" one boy put in. "They wouldn't accept you in the *Luftwaffe*. You're much too fat. You wouldn't even fit into a Stuka."

Offended, Otto turned away.

A little boy took advantage of the pause to say in a determined voice: "I'll become a staff officer. Staff officers are made generals more quickly than others. And it's quite safe. And how the girls will run after me when I go walking down the street with red stripes down my pants, red coat lapels, gold buttons, and golden braiding—and the Iron Cross dangling from my collar."

"Will you listen to that coward!'" his neighbor said indignantly. "Quite safe, he says, and he thinks he'll get the Iron Cross on top of a cushy job." He tipped his index finger to his forehead. "Just think a minute. By the time you're promoted to staff officer, years will have passed—and the war will have been over for ages."

Heinz still couldn't make himself heard.

"I'm going into the navy!" another boy was shouting. "Submarines, that's the thing. Always under water around England. Not a single ship will reach the island. In the last world war they did the same to us. And they can't live more than a fortnight without supplies from the outside, you know. Those bastards over there, they'll starve to death; they'll be glad to eat the dirt off the floor. We treated the Polacks much too well. When we march into England, we won't have anything left to do but shovel the earth over the bodies to stop the stench. And then *we'll* colonize England!"

"Stop it!" Heinz shouted. "Enough!"

But one boy who hadn't announced his plan yet paid no attention. He turned to the submariner. "What do you get out of it, always being under water? You don't see anything! I'm going into the army, and when we march into France I'll wipe out every Frenchman in sight!" Raising an imaginary rifle to firing position, he aimed at us and started banging away around the room. "My old man wants to come along with me. He really hates the French because they shot off the little finger on his left hand in 1917. And there are beautiful girls in France; my old man told me about them. Just think how they'll run after us when there aren't any more dirty Frenchmen around. They are crazy about men, you know, especially blond German men." He tittered. "They also have enough wine for everybody, my old man says. And then our victory will be celebrated! I tell you, that'll be a life!" He smacked his lips loudly.

Nobody knew how to outdo him.

"Where's Heinz?" a boy asked suddenly.

Everyone looked at Heinz's place beside Günther. It was empty. Heinz had gone.

"Gone," Otto said, "but who cares!"

Günther sat motionless in his place. His chin was low on his chest, his eyes were closed.

"Hey, Günther! You asleep?" Otto nudged him. "You

haven't said anything yet! Come on, what do you want to be in the war?"

Günther sat up with a start. Contemptuously he looked around. Then he leaped off the table. He walked to the door, turned back to face us. Softly he said, "Your grave-digger, you pigs!" and left the room.

VIII
-1940-

The Party

Heinz, Günther, and I were spending the afternoon in our *Heim,* intending to sort and rearrange our library.

Since the campaign in Norway, Heinz was expecting to receive his call-up papers any day, and he wanted to arrange everything so that his successor could take over without any difficulties.

It was hard to get an overview of the contents of the library. We had five volumes of Adolf Hitler's *Mein Kampf;* they stood pristine and untouched on the shelves, their pages still stuck together. On the other hand, *The Hitler Boy Quex, Ghosts at the Dead Man,* and *Wanderer Between Two Worlds* were almost always out.

It was easy work.

Günther took the books off the shelves. I dusted them off. Heinz wrote out new cards for them. Then we all made new covers out of black paper Günther had managed to get from somewhere. We were just debating whether *Folk Without Space* was worth re-covering—it had been read to tatters—when there was a knock on the door.

"Come in!" Heinz called without looking up.

"Heil Hitler!"

Only when we heard the voice did we look up in surprise. In the doorway stood a platoon leader of the *Bund Deutscher Mädel*. She was slim, had blue eyes, and wore her light blonde hair gathered into a knot at the nape of her neck.

I liked her.

One could see Günther's admiration in his eyes.

Heinz jumped up.

"My name's Hede," the girl began, confidently steering toward Heinz. "Are you Heinz?"

Heinz nodded.

She held her hand out over the table and said, "You were recommended to me. I need your help."

Günther fetched a chair and wiped it with his handkerchief.

Hede sat down without being asked. She went right on talking. "Together with the older girls in my group, I want to give a farewell party for the soldiers who'll be leaving for the front soon. We have a small hall. We wanted to ask if you could detail us two or three boys to help decorate it?"

"Of course!" Heinz assured her, "of course!" He looked at me and Günther. "Is it all right with you if we three come?"

"That's fine by me," Hede said, and smiled.

"Oh, but we can't!" Heinz remembered with annoyance. "We are all going on a training course for Hitler Youth wardens the day after tomorrow, and it lasts ten days. What a pity."

"But that doesn't matter," Hede said. "The party's not until next month. You'll have time."

"Fine!" Günther was delighted. "We'll come."

Hede got up. "See you in two weeks then. I'll let you know where and when."

We clicked our heels together and bowed as she shook hands with each of us.

I opened the door for her. She turned when she reached it and said, "And naturally you'll join in the festivities!"

The plan was Heinz's.

I brought my large electricity kit.

Günther brought his father's heavy toolbox.

Heinz carried a fat briefcase.

Hede greeted us joyfully. She was getting the hall ready, together with three other girl leaders. One of them served us sandwiches and hot chocolate.

We began our work with a coffee klatsch.

I felt better than usual and tried to show my best side.

Günther shone. One joke after the other succeeded; again and again he made the girls laugh.

Without admitting it to each other, we knew we were all three in love—and all three in love with Hede.

It was least noticeable with Heinz. But his eyes followed her around, he kept smiling to himself, and he found it difficult to tear himself away.

But we finally did begin our work.

Heinz climbed a ladder. He stretched bell-wire from wall to wall along the ceiling and connected small colored bulbs. Then he covered everything with colored crepe paper.

Meanwhile, Günther tapped the electrical circuit. Screening it, he laid a cable from the meter to a little room off the hall. I sat in this room and rigged up a primitive instrument panel.

"Can't be a large unit that's being seen off here," Günther said as he came into the room.

"Well, then, just look around," I said, pointing to the corner behind my work table.

There lay row upon row of wine bottles, and next to them stood brandy and champagne. Cans of meat and fish, hefty chunks of cheese, and several packages of real butter were stacked ready for the feast. Two sausages, each as long as an arm, hung from the ceiling.

"Wow!" exclaimed Günther. "And to think we live on rations!" He looked back into the hall. "That room holds thirty at most, so who's supposed to eat and drink all that?"

"Perhaps we can take home whatever's left over!" I said hopefully.

Günther didn't answer.

When Heinz had finished with his part of the work, we connected everything up, tested it one more time, and asked the girls to sit down.

Heinz closed the drapes.

The girls were examining the ceiling decorations with curiosity. The room illuminations blazed up. The colored paper made things look warm and comfortable. The girls nodded contentedly.

Very slowly I turned down the lights. A kind of twilight settled over the room.

"Ah," said the girls.

Suddenly the little bulbs over the dance floor lit up like a skyful of stars.

The girls were ecstatic.

Günther put a dance record onto the record player in the corner. As the music softly filled the room, the tiny lights over the dance floor kept flickering on and off.

The girls applauded.

Our surprise had worked.

A little shyly, Heinz went over to Hede and asked her to dance.

They danced till the end of the record.

As a reward for our accomplishment, the girls stood us to another round of sausage and cheese sandwiches. They even gave each of us a bottle of beer.

While we were eating, the three other girls said goodbye.

Only Hede remained.

Heinz was beaming at her and almost forgot to chew.

"I'll do the last few things myself," Hede was saying.

"May I help you?" Heinz asked.

Hede nodded.

Günther nudged me unobtrusively and gave me a look. We stood up. "You won't mind if we go on ahead home, will you!" Günther said.

Heinz appeared in a freshly ironed uniform.

Günther and I had also put on our best clothes.

As we entered the room, Hede didn't even shake hands with us.

Puzzled, we stood by the entrance.

"Go to your switchboard and stay in that room!" Hede demanded.

Taken aback, we looked at each other.

"Why?" Günther asked. "I thought we were invited."

"Have the girls give you something!" Hede said and turned away.

We were speechless.

"She's just very nervous," said Heinz, trying to sound consoling. He walked ahead of us to the back room.

A girl was already at work there. Wearing an apron, she was buttering slices of bread, placing meat and cheese on them, and arranging the open sandwiches colorfully on large platters.

We said hello to each other and stood next to her.

"Please don't take anything off the platters!" she begged. Quickly she filled three rolls with sausage for us.

Heinz didn't feel hungry.

The Party

Günther and I shared his roll.

"She looks terrific tonight!" Heinz said.

"Yes. Well put together," Günther agreed, chewing.

The girl next to us smiled but said nothing.

We examined our set-up once more, then looked out into the hall.

There girls were restlessly running back and forth. Again and again they would stop in front of a little mirror in the corner and pull straight their white blouses or comb their hair. Then they would hasten to the door and peer outside. Shortly afterward they'd turn back to the tables, rearrange a chair, push a flower into better light.

"Nothing but leaders!" Günther remarked.

"No mere girl ever gets to take part in these parties," the girl with the apron said without being asked. "We are only good enough to help with the preparations," she added.

In the larger room Hede was welcoming the first guest, a young second lieutenant.

Now all the girls surrounded the officer; they laughed and glowed. When he began to tell a story, they listened with sparkling eyes.

But just then Hede took the young lieutenant's arm. Leaving the other leaders by the door, she led her guest around the room.

Shortly afterward the second guest, a first lieutenant, arrived. With a smile, Hede excused herself and handed the second lieutenant over to another leader. She turned toward the new arrival. She linked arms with him and led him through the room in the same way she had his predecessor. But she could only give him a moment.

Two captains had now arrived.

"Nothing but officers so far!" Günther said in astonishment.

"They don't bother with privates and noncommissioned officers," the girl in the apron explained.

Hede gave the two captains the same tour of the room. This time she got as far as our room.

We heard her explain, "Those are our storage and kitchen facilities."

One captain wanted to look inside.

Hede pushed the door open all the way.

And the captain saw us. "What kind of milksops do you have here?" he asked.

Heinz shot up from his chair.

"To fetch and carry and clean up," Hede replied, quickly pulling her captains away from the room.

Heinz's face had turned a pasty color. He had sunk back onto the chair and hunched over.

Without saying a word, Günther took out a screwdriver and started to disconnect the switchboard from the mains.

"You can't do that!" Heinz protested.

"Who says I can't?" said Günther without interrupting his work.

"But we promised to help!" Heinz reminded him.

"Not under these circumstances!" Günther replied. To the girl in the apron he said, "You have some fine leader!"

The girl shrugged.

Heinz tried to take the screwdriver away from Günther.

"If you don't let me disconnect this," Günther threatened, "I'll black out the whole works, but in such a way that the whole party will be canceled. Let the pretty Hede see where she gets someone to clean up."

When Günther had severed all the connections, he turned the switchboard over to me.

"What do you think?" Heinz asked me helplessly.

"I think we should leave!" I said.

"And we will leave right now!" Günther ordered simply. Heinz gave in.

"Thanks for the hospitality and Auf Wiedersehen," Günther said to the girl making sandwiches.

"What you're doing is right," she said. "But I'm the one who loses out. Who'll help me uncork all those bottles now?"

Günther grabbed a cheese sandwich off the table.

In single file we marched out of our room and through the hall. The officers regarded us in puzzlement.

At the door Hede caught up with us. "But you can't leave us in the lurch like this!"

Heinz turned his back to her.

"Try us!" Günther said soberly. "It's still too early to clean up anyway!"

The Successor

"At attention!"

We stood to attention.

Only one person in the back rank was out of step.

The eyes of the new *Gefolgschaftsführer* slowly drifted over the unit and stopped at our platoon.

Expectantly we drew ourselves up straighter.

"Heinz and Günther, step forward!"

In a few steps Heinz walked to the *Gefolgschaftsführer* from his place in the flank of the platoon.

Günther was in the second rank. Stepping back out of the platoon, he had to run round the whole unit to get to the leader. Then he stood shoulder to shoulder with Heinz.

The two had their backs turned toward us. At a gesture from the leader, they wheeled far enough around to be able to see us as well.

Smiling, Heinz bit down on his lower lip.

Günther looked at us questioningly.

"The first part of the drive in the West has been successfully concluded," the *Gefolgschaftsführer* began. "The second, perhaps most difficult, part is still ahead of us. We must not conclude from the retreat of the English at Dunkirk that they will surrender their island as easily. The victory over England will require great efforts—and sacrifices. For this mission our Führer needs every man." He hesitated and looked down.

Behind me someone began to grumble that we had to listen to the speech at attention.

"Many of us have already hastened to the colors," the Hitler Youth leader continued. "Many have already been killed in action or been wounded on the battlefield. Of our *Gefolgschaft,* five comrades so far have died the hero's death. My predecessor here lies buried in French soil." He fell silent for a moment. "But we must not remain in mourning. We must continue along the path until the Final Victory of the Greater German Reich."

Now he turned toward Heinz.

Heinz stood even straighter.

The leader clasped his shoulders and pushed him one step forward. "Now one of our best platoon leaders has volunteered for military service. Heinz has asked me to release him from duty until his call-up. We will therefore take our leave of him here and now." He took Heinz's hand. "Heinz, I thank you. You were a good Hitler Youth and an exemplary platoon leader. Now become a courageous soldier of our Führer. We all wish you good luck."

"Thank you, sir," Heinz replied softly and stepped back.

His superior went on, "Together we have debated who would be best suited to take over the orphaned platoon. Heinz himself has proposed a successor. I have confidence in his judgment and believe he has chosen the right man." He turned toward Günther.

Günther still wore his most stupid expression.

Heinz pushed him toward the *Gefolgschaftsführer.*

"With the agreement of the state leader, I hereby name you, Günther, the new platoon leader. I hope you will continue to lead the platoon in Heinz's image."

Günther looked dazedly from the *Gefolgschaftsführer* to Heinz. He let both shake his hand.

"Why Günther of all people?" muttered Otto.

Heinz unfastened the cord of his office and attached it to Günther's uniform. But Günther still looked as if he hadn't grasped what had happened.

Heinz led him to our platoon and placed him in the platoon leader's position.

In closing we sang:

> "A young folk stands ready, ready for the storm!
> Raise the banners high, comrades.
> We can feel our time approaching,
> the time of the young soldiers.
> Before us march with tattered flags
> the dead heroes of the young nation,
> and above us our heroic ancestors.
> Germany, Fatherland, we're on our way!"

Shortly thereafter the *Gefolgschaftsführer* dismissed us. When we were alone, Günther asked: "Why did you do that, Heinz? You know what I think about all this. I'm not a real Hitler Youth—and I'm certainly not a real leader."

Heinz laid both hands on Günther's shoulders. He looked at him a long time. Then he pointed with his head to the spot where the whole *Gefolgschaft* had stood. "Do you know who among them is better suited? Do you want the perfumed one back? They need a leader who will assume responsibility for his orders."

The Parting

It was drafty in the enormous railroad station. Rain dripped through a broken pane in the roof. Arriving trains thundered in, departing trains hissed through the station.

On the narrow strip between platforms five and six, hundreds of people were jammed together.

In the middle young men were crowded together. They carried cardboard boxes or had placed them by their feet. Most looked as if they had spent a sleepless night. Four black, white, and red posts hemmed them in.

An army of mothers, women, and children was surging around the young soldiers. They kept pushing as far as the barrier, were forced to retreat, and advanced again. A few tried to slip underneath the rope, and only the warning cry of a neighbor ultimately held them back. Then they'd content themselves with asking for "Philip" or "Martin."

Among those in the middle, the name would run from mouth to mouth, and somewhere an arm would lift and wave. And a woman would dance on her toes and happily wave a handkerchief over her head.

Only rarely did anyone from the inside manage to get as far as the rope. But when he did, a mother, a wife, a girl would at once hasten to the spot. Then they'd bend backward and forward, embrace, kiss.

The immediate neighbors inside the barrier could not turn away. There was no space to turn around in, and in any case, two others were clinging tightly together on their other side.

The women on the far side of the barrier looked to the

ground in embarrassment and dabbed at the corners of their eyes.

A sergeant major was circling the roped-off square without a pause. He separated with force those saying good-bye.

Behind his back, those he had separated gave each other a last kiss, whispered something, and finally could do nothing but wave and throw kisses at each other.

"Mother!" a light voice called out. "Mother!" A boy tried to break out of the pen. Pitilessly, the sergeant major pushed him back. "Get a hold on yourself, man!" he bellowed.

"I think it's time," Heinz said. He looked at the station clock and changed the cardboard box from his right to his left hand.

"And your father and mother, aren't they coming?" Günther asked.

Heinz shook his head. "I asked them not to. We said good-bye at home. That's better than in front of everybody here on the platform."

"That's true," Günther agreed.

Heinz shook hands with us. "I hope I can come back to you soon. I wish you all the best meanwhile. And you, Günther, don't let the platoon down. Promise me!"

To me he said, "Keep your eye on him so he won't get into mischief!" Then he took his call-up papers from his pocket.

"All the best, Heinz, and a safe homecoming!"

Heinz smiled at us and walked over to the sergeant major.

"You sure took your time!" the sergeant major barked at him.

"The train hasn't arrived yet," Heinz replied.

The sergeant major took a deep breath. "If you start out like this, you'll have a whole lot of fun with us!"

Without looking at the sergeant major, Heinz bent down and slipped underneath the rope to join the other captives.

"You fine young gentlemen of the Hitler Youth, you really think you can claim special privileges here!" the sergeant major bawled after Heinz.

Günther had turned away and was staring at the vaulted ceiling of the station. Now he turned back, his eyelids slightly red.

When the waiting women opened up the view for a moment, he waved at Heinz. Heinz nodded.

"Stand back all!" The voice of the sergeant major thundered through the station.

The station mistress in her red cap and carrying a green-rimmed signal appeared on the platform.

The train rumbled onto Platform 5.

With his arms outstretched, the sergeant major kept the platform between the train and the roped-off men free. He unknotted the rope at one post and in a resounding voice counted off the shoving young men.

Two corporals led those who had been counted to compartments.

Then the sergeant major marched briskly up and down in front of the steps. He motioned the two corporals into the train. No one was allowed to approach the cars. Those who had been loaded onto them burst out of the small window openings.

We couldn't find Heinz.

"Papa! Papa!" cried a little girl. "Papa!" rang shrilly through the station.

Suddenly all the women were sobbing. No one was ashamed, no one hid her tears.

The white signal with the green rim was raised. Two shrieks from the whistle. The train pulled slowly out of the station.

The sergeant major was the last to jump aboard.

Fragments of a hiking song drifted thinly back to us.

"All the best!" Günther shouted after the disappearing train.

Behind on the platform were sobbing mothers, wives, girls, and children, and here and there an old man.

By the stairs at the exit, Heinz's parents were looking after the train. Both were crying.

IX
-1941-

Bringing in the Harvest

The farmer was kneeling in a field. With a hoe the size of a small hand, he went around a group of tiny plants and pulled up three. Only one, with two small leaves, remained standing.

"That's how you do it!"

We gaped and nodded.

He held one of the pulled plants toward us. "All these have to come out; only one stays in the ground."

We were in agreement.

"What kind of weed is that?" asked one member of our harvest squad.

The farmer sank from his knees onto the seat of his

pants. Dumbfounded, he regarded the questioner. "You don't know what that is?"

"Do *you* know anything about weeds?" the boy asked Günther.

The farmer leaped up. Despairingly he shouted: "Whoever sent you to help with the harvest wants to bring me to the grave!" And he flung the little hoe onto the ground, where it stuck fast. "Those aren't weeds, you dumb-dumb, those are turnips, excess turnips!" The boy looked at the farmer in disbelief.

"But turnips are this thick!" he said, indicating the size of a head.

"Yes," groaned the farmer, "when we harvest them, they are indeed that thick. But till then they have to grow. And so that they may grow without hindrance, you are supposed to pull out—"

"Oh, that's why!"

Sighing, the farmer gave up. "Here, each of you take on two rows at a time." He handed each a little hoe. "One farm worker does the whole field in a morning, so I imagine ten of you can get it done by lunchtime. Then you bring the tools back to me and you are free to go home." He picked up his bicycle, cast a last glance over his field, and left, muttering: "Poor turnips!"

"And this on a Sunday!" protested Otto. "Under Heinz we never had to do things like this!"

"True," Günther agreed, "there wasn't any harvest duty then. But soldiers also have to fight on Sundays—and this way we do our part on the home front."

Before us lay the field, row beside row, one tiny turnip plant after the other.

"Well, let's get started!" Günther commanded.

Each of us squatted down between two rows. We began to weed out the excess turnips. It wasn't as easy as we had thought. If you didn't aim precisely, you'd uproot everything.

Günther was sliding along two rows away from me. He was deeply absorbed in his work; he neither talked nor looked up.

I took a lot of trouble over the little plants I pulled up by mistake. I'd search out the least damaged one and replant it in the ground. I lost a lot of time that way.

At the end of the first pair of rows, Günther gave us a short break. He waited until everyone had finished his rows so we could start on the new ones at the same time.

What monotonous work! Right, left, slide forward. Right, left, forward. And right, left, forward, right, left....

When I raised my head, I couldn't estimate the length of my rows. A look backward was disappointing. How little I had done, how much more remained to be done!

After his second pair of rows Otto complained of hunger.

The rest went on working.

Otto sat down at the edge of the field and ate his sandwiches.

The unfamiliar bent position strained the small of my back. And ahead of me turnips, nothing but turnips. . . .

"I give up!" one boy declared after his fourth round. "My arm's lame!"

Günther shrugged in resignation and worked on. The boy's example found imitators. One after the other reported unfit for work.

It was contagious. I, too, thought I could hardly move my arm any more. My back ached. I already saw red blotches on the palms of my hands.

There were four of us left. At the next round we were three. The third stopped halfway through his pair of rows.

"Can one of you finish off his two rows?" Günther asked the boys sitting at the side of the field.

"We are tired," came the reply.

Otto's voice was the loudest.

Günther and I divided up the unfinished work. The others sat in a circle telling jokes.

Only two more rounds for each.

I crept along between my rows. Sometimes I applied the hoe so weakly I only scratched the ground but didn't remove any turnip seedlings. Then I'd have to repeat the motion. I felt like lying down in the field and staying there.

"We were supposed to be finished by lunchtime!" Otto called to us. "And it's already half-past two!"

Finally we had done it. It was good to stand up and walk. Rivulets of sweat ran down our two dusty faces.

"Why don't you go on ahead!" Günther told the waiting group. "I'm going to return the hoes."

They started off at once.

I helped Günther carry the tools. On the way I examined my blisters. "Do you have some too?" I asked Günther.

He showed me his hand.

"But those are blood blisters!"

"I had simple blisters after the third round," he said with a smile.

Heroes

Heinz sat enthroned on the table in his gray field uniform. He had placed his feet, clad in short black boots, on a chair. Silver braiding decorated his shoulder straps. A black-white-red ribbon adorned the placket of his battle-dress tunic. He carried his left hand in a narrow black sling.

The whole platoon had turned up, including those who never had time usually. There were also some boys from a different platoon who knew Heinz from the past. They all wanted to share this visit.

Günther had told everyone we were expecting Heinz. He wanted him to have a magnificent reception. And now we were admiring Heinz, his insignia of rank, his wounded arm, his decorations.

"Do we have to call you 'sir' now?" Otto asked.

Heinz shook his head, smiling.

"Come on, Heinz," said Otto, "tell us something beautiful about the war!"

Heinz turned serious at once. "There isn't much to tell and nothing that's 'beautiful.' War is a dirty business!"

A nagging voice in the background said, "Why did you

come here then if you don't want to tell us anything?"

Otto called out: "Don't worry! Nothing but false modesty!"

Heinz didn't reply directly. "What do you want to hear then?"

"Something about heroes!" one of the younger boys suggested.

Again, Heinz smiled. "You and your heroes! I've only met one hero so far, a real hero! And he was quite different from the kind you imagine!"

"Tell!" came from all sides.

"What's his name?" Otto wanted to know. "Do we know him? Has he been named in the *Wehrmacht* bulletin?"

"Neither—nor!" answered Heinz. "This hero remains utterly unknown. He has never received a medal. He didn't even die at the front."

"A good spy then?" speculated the boy.

"No," Heinz assured him, "a very simple, insignificant corporal, but a hero!"

"Tell!"

Heinz hesitated a moment longer. Then he began:

"In my training outfit there were several groups of older men apart from us boys. All family men, fathers of five and six children. They were to be trained only for guard duty at home.

"The instructors took it easy with these men. Usually they took them out to the training area in the morning, laid low in a little wood and played cards with them until their duty period was over. If any officer entered the area, the cards disappeared and the instructors would casually explain some drill or other. And because the officers weren't very happy at having to bother with these heads of families either, nothing ever happened.

"Only one of the instructors took his job seriously. This was a corporal who had been shot in the left hand during the French campaign. Apparently he could no longer close his hand. Most considered him a malingerer who didn't want to go to the front. He was all alone, and he had no friends. Unlike other group leaders, he never sat down with his men at night. As soon as duty was over, he disappeared.

"He spent most of his off-duty time in a bar. A real loner. No one liked him, and his men feared him and hated him.

"One day this corporal was supposed to drill his men in throwing live hand grenades. He took them to a makeshift firing range. The duty officer went along as supervisor but paid little attention to the actual drill.

"The corporal took his older men over the safety precautions once more. He gave precise and strict instructions about how they were to handle the grenades: pull the pin —swing it back as far as possible—throw it away! Then he went into the hole with the first man, sending the others into cover.

"The man ripped out the pin. But instead of throwing the grenade away and lying down, he ran back into cover with it in hand. The corporal behind him shouted: 'Throw it away!' He tried to smash the grenade out of the man's hand. Then the man threw it—but he threw it into the cover.

"The men screamed out in horror.

"At the last moment, the corporal flung himself flat onto the grenade. He was dead at once.

"The old chaps didn't get so much as a splinter."

Heinz said nothing for a while.

We, too, kept quiet.

"That was a hero!" Heinz finished his story. "The only hero I have seen so far."

Premilitary Training

"So you're the Hitler boys!" he greeted us, regarding us suspiciously. "And I'm to turn you into human beings!"

Somewhat intimidated, we huddled around the big table in the barracks and looked at him.

He shouldered his rifle and limped up and down in front of us. "No, no," he lamented, "what an honest veteran staff sergeant is expected to do nowadays!" He sadly shook his head. "Now I have to play nursemaid as well!"

We didn't know how to behave.

But he regained control of himself and sighed, "Well, orders are orders, so I'll train you for military service." He emphasized the word "military" somewhat, making it sound ridiculous. "I'll train you because 'a soldier finds his highest reward and greatest happiness in the realization of gladly fulfilled duty.' "

He stood straight, pulled the rifle butt toward him, took off the rifle in one sharp movement, and propped it up against one of the bunks. Then he looked at us more kindly.

We returned his smile.

"Won't be so bad!" he assured us. "I think we'll get along for the fortnight."

We nodded hopefully.

He pulled a stool out from under the table and joined us. "Well, let's begin then! And what do we start with?" He looked at each of us in turn. "We start with the most important thing for every soldier. Who knows what it is?"

We stared at him dumbly.

He raised his eyes to the ceiling and groaned, "How did I deserve this? You don't even know that? 'The most important thing in the life of every soldier is his bride.' "

Otto grinned.

"Not the bride you have in mind!" the staff sergeant told Otto. "The soldier's bride is this!" He picked up the rifle and flung it on the table in front of us.

We started back in fright.

"This is a *Karabiner 98k*. But don't imagine you can treat it in the same fashion. 'It is the special duty of every soldier to get to know his weapons thoroughly and to follow instructions about their cleaning and handling meticulously'! And you don't throw your bride around!"

Behind the scolding and the shouting hid a smile; we began to like our staff sergeant.

"Now I want to know what you can do." He turned to Günther. "You're the leader of this lot?"

Günther jumped up. "Yes, sir!"

The staff sergeant made a face. "No need to be that sharp! Upsets my stomach. Don't forget, this isn't the Hitler Youth."

Günther bit on his lower lip to keep back the smile and stood at ease.

But we all laughed.

"Here, show me what you can do!" the staff sergeant said to Günther. He pushed the rifle across to him. "Show these boys here how to take that thing apart."

Günther looked aghast. He carefully lifted the rifle with the tips of his fingers.

The staff sergeant nudged the boy sitting closest to him. "Go on, run to the supply room and give the sergeant a nice hello from me! And ask him to please send over a pair of white gloves for a young gentleman who would like to take a rifle apart!"

The boy raced to the door. Only then did he realize the order hadn't been serious. He blushed and looked at Günther.

"Careful now," the staff sergeant was warning Günther. "If you wait any longer, the rifle'll fall apart by itself— from old age!" He got up and limped out of the room.

Sitting next to Günther, I pulled up the bolt handle and opened the breech.

Günther accidentally pulled at the lock support, and the lock clattered onto the table.

The staff sergeant turned back to us at once. "I am frightened. I fear you've already turned the rifle into salad. What do I see? You didn't even manage to take the lock apart!"

Back at the table he said, "This is taking too long for me! Hand it over!"

Disappointed in himself, Günther handed the rifle and lock to the staff sergeant.

With a few deft movements, the sergeant stripped the rifle and arranged its parts neatly on the table. He told us the name and use of each part.

We gaped at them.

"Who trusts himself to put this thing back together again?" he asked.

Otto raised his hand without hesitation.

The staff sergeant mixed up the parts thoroughly and pushed them over to Otto, who speedily and skillfully re-assembled the rifle and handed it to the staff sergeant.

"I'll be damned!" the staff sergeant said. "Where did you learn that?"

"Paid attention, that's all!" Otto replied.

"Five more rounds for each!" the captain decided. "I want to see what infant prodigy strayed in with you." He stood behind the platform and watched the target through binoculars.

We pushed close behind the captain and waited with bated breath.

A few had bet against the staff sergeant.

Günther flipped a ten-pfennig piece.

The staff sergeant won and went first. His face was twisted in a grimace of pain as he raised his leg onto the platform and pulled himself up after it. He laid the rifle down on the sand sack and loaded it.

From behind the backstop the signal for "Fire!" was held up.

The staff sergeant calmly took aim.

"Remember your marksmanship award, sergeant," the captain said.

The staff sergeant gave no reply. Very deliberately he lowered the gun barrel. His index finger curled around the trigger. He fired.

"Eleven, aimed to the right!" the staff sergeant reported, and put down the rifle.

Everyone looked toward the backstop. The target disappeared, and right afterward the scoreboard was held up: "Twelve!"

The staff sergeant shouted the result to a soldier who wrote it down after repeating it.

"Good," said the captain.

"Ten, aimed low," the staff sergeant reported next.

"Ten low" the board showed.

The staff sergeant went on to shoot a ten, an eleven, and another twelve.

"Very good!" the captain declared with satisfaction. "What's the total score?" he asked the recording soldier.

"Fifty-five, sir!"

Laughing, the staff sergeant rolled himself off the platform. "Now it's your turn," he told Otto. "If you shoot fifty-five or better, I'll treat you to a bottle tonight!"

Otto jumped onto the sand sack.

"You shot for the first time today?" the captain inquired.

"No, sir!" replied Otto. "When I was younger, I often tried in a shooting gallery."

The captain laughed. "Can't call that shooting! I mean, you really held a real rifle in your hand for the first time today?"

"Yes, sir!"

On the whole firing range not a single person believed Otto could touch the staff sergeant.

Otto leveled the gun. He took aim at once. The shot rang out.

"Announce score!" the recording soldier called out.

Otto still didn't put down the rifle. "Didn't see!" he finally admitted in a meek voice.

The captain and the staff sergeant exchanged glances.

Sure of victory, the staff sergeant smiled.

"Nine low!" the board showed up ahead.

A bit scornfully, the captain pushed out his lower lip.

For his second shot, Otto took longer to aim. "Twelve!" he announced.

The shot actually sat fast in the tenth circle.

"Twelve, aimed high!" Otto announced next.

Again the captain and the staff sergeant smiled at each other.

"Eleven low!" the board showed.

"Eleven high!" Otto shouted.

Twelve!

And again: "Eleven high!"

Twelve!

"Good, good," acknowledged the captain. "The final score?"

"Fifty-four, sir!" the recording soldier announced.

"Really remarkable!" the captain said, slapping Otto on the shoulder. "Boy, you are an excellent rifleman!"

Otto beamed. With one bound he was off the platform and standing at attention.

"My congratulations on your achievement." The captain took Otto's hand and pumped it enthusiastically.

In the meantime the staff sergeant had lifted the rifle off the sand sack. He started, then walked over to the captain. "Sir, I have something important to report!"

"Go ahead!" said the captain, interrupting his conversation with Otto.

"The boy forgot to adjust the sight for distance. He has fired all his shots with sight 100."

The captain looked at Otto. "That shouldn't have happened. But it proves the boy really is a first-class rifleman. If you take that into consideration when you look at the score, Sergeant, you must admit he's really a *better* shot than you!"

"Yes, sir!" acknowledged the staff sergeant. "He did better than I did!"

"We must write and tell Heinz," Günther said to us.

Everyone participated in the letter-writing. Everyone had

something to report, had a question to ask or a request to make.

Günther was already filling the third page when the door quietly opened.

We looked up.

The staff sergeant pushed his head through the opening. Before Günther could jump up and shout "Attention!" the staff sergeant said, "Go on with what you are doing!"

We stayed where we were.

Only now did our visitor come in. He was carrying a bottle and a brandy glass. "I need a stool," he declared as he walked to the table, dragging one foot behind him.

Otto was already behind him, stool in hand.

"A promise is a promise," the staff sergeant said as he put the bottle on the table. "Nothing special, just my last ration of German brandy. But I only own one glass, so go and get out your mugs. And you, Otto, come sit by me."

We took our mugs and glasses from the lockers while the staff sergeant uncorked the bottle and poured himself a shot.

Otto had brought a cup.

The staff sergeant judged each portion by eye. Then he raised his glass. "To the best rifleman in our training course!"

Otto blushed.

We drank, coughed, some spit.

Otto poured the contents of his cup down in one gulp.

"And you want to become soldiers!" the staff sergeant reprimanded us. "Can't even stomach a sip of Schnapps!

Take Otto here for an example; he not only shoots well, he also drinks like a fish. He'll make some soldier!"

"That stuff doesn't taste good, and it scratches my throat," one boy complained.

"Could be, but you had better get used to it. Although it's not included in the curriculum, it's really part of 'premilitary training.' Because soldiers who don't drink can't stomach life at the front. Believe you me, boys!"

We said nothing in reply. A few tried the brandy once more.

"Are you writing a book?" the staff sergeant asked, turning to Günther.

"No," Günther replied, "we're writing a joint letter to our former platoon leader."

The staff sergeant gave us all another drink. "What's he doing now?"

"He's at the Eastern Front, in the northern section. He's a sergeant," Otto said.

"Poor cow!" the staff sergeant commented. "He'll freeze to death. Hope the same thing that happened to me doesn't happen to him."

"Do you also have injuries from frostbite?" we asked.

"Well," he said, "first they shoot me in the knee. And as I'm lying there waiting for help, my toes go and freeze off as well."

"Do they ever heal up completely?"

"Who knows? I reckon they'll send me out to the front again next year."

"What do you think of the situation at the Russian front?" Otto inquired.

"*Think,* boy? Better not to think! If I *thought* about the Eastern Front I'd go crazy. My feeling is we should never have started in Russia. It's not as simple as in Poland or France. The country's too big." He raised his glass and drank.

"But we'll be victorious all the same!" one boy threw in.

Our staff sergeant looked at him in disbelief but said nothing. He divided up the rest of the bottle. "To our course!" he toasted as he got up.

We, too, stood and drank.

"Finish your letter. Till tomorrow!" he said, and limped out of the room.

X

-1942-

The Attack

When the sirens wailed, I jumped out of bed. As fast as I could, I slipped into my uniform, put the air-raid helmet on, and pulled on my boots.

My mother allowed herself more time to get dressed.

Father stayed in bed until the last moment.

Mother caught me at the door. "Here, take this," she said, handing me a sandwich. "You never know how long it'll take!" When I was already on the stairs, she called after me: "Take care, boy! Look after yourself!"

On the main floor Frau Resch, the wife of our landlord, was already setting suitcases outside their apartment door. She had to get over to the public air-raid shelter; her husband was the warden there.

The Attack

The stars glittered, but there was no moon. It was a lovely spring night. The trees smelled sweet. A few old people were already scurrying to the nearest shelter with their small suitcases and their pocketbooks.

Still nothing could be heard. A single searchlight had been trained against the sky.

If you looked carefully, you could make out shreds of light around the rims of the blackout curtains in almost every home. Everyone was making preparations to dash down to the cellar or the nearest air-raid shelter at the first bark of the antiaircraft guns.

Calmly I followed the same path I had taken so many nights before. Each of those nights had passed harmlessly. For almost a month the bombers had spared our town.

Shortly before I reached our *Heim,* I heard the droning in the air. Quickly it increased.

All the antiaircraft guns started blasting away simultaneously. When they discovered an enemy bomber, they enclosed it in bundles of light. Gliding along in their strong light, the airplane tried to break away, climbed, dove, wavered. But the guns found their target—until a flash and a dull rumble of thunder signaled the end. Wings and body tumbled over and over, and the searchlights looked for new targets.

Because the air buzzed with falling fragments, I went and stood in a house entrance. From there I watched the drama in the sky. But when the rain of splinters grew thicker, and the jagged red-hot iron pieces kept bouncing up from the pavement, I retreated back as far as the hallway.

The street was empty.

The chinks between blackout curtains and window frames no longer showed any light. Everything was dark. Only the reflection of the fireworks in the sky illuminated houses, streets, and trees.

Behind me the last tenants in the house hastened down the steps to the cellar. They were very nervous. "Today we'll get it!" I heard one man say breathlessly.

Then I was alone once more. I had only to cross the street to reach the *Heim,* where the others were waiting for me. But now bombers were flying overhead in formation. My head began to reverberate with the droning of the many planes. I huddled into myself; I was afraid.

At that moment there was a rushing sound above me.

I flung myself to the ground.

The rushing sound grew louder.

I pressed against the wall.

The rushing drowned out the noise of the planes and the thunder of the artillery.

I trembled.

A hit!

Then nothing! Nothing but the droning and the barking of guns.

No collapsed walls! No dust!

Only a crackling!

I looked up.

Incendiary bombs!

"Everything's burning!" I shouted into the cellar of our meeting house.

The Attack

They sat huddled, pale, tired. Günther raised one shoulder. "We haven't had any operational orders."

I sat down by them.

No one felt like talking. Cowed, our heads ducked down, we listened to what was going on outside. Our cellar walls muffled the sounds.

"Only Otto's missing," Günther said a while later.

"He probably overslept," one boy suggested.

"Perhaps he stopped off in a cellar on the way," I said.

At that moment a new group of bombers flew over us. The cellar walls vibrated. The antiaircraft fire made the whole building shake.

There. A whistling sound!

We made ourselves small.

A hit somewhere close by.

The whole cellar rose and sank down again.

A boy who'd been asleep in the corner fell off his bench.

The lights went out.

The cellar door flew open.

"Damn!" someone swore.

"Light!" cried another.

Everyone was searching for matches.

At last the first candle was lit.

The door was closed.

Bomber formation after bomber formation flew over us.

"Those at the front are better off," Günther remarked. "At least Heinz can defend himself when the others attack. But we have to sit here and take it all without protest. It's enough to drive you nuts! Sit, wait, unable to do anything —and the whole sky full of bombers!"

Suddenly one of the little ones leaped off his bench. He raced to the door.

"Where do you think you're going?" Günther asked, holding the door shut with his foot.

The little boy howled: "Let me out! I want my mother! Let me out!" He kicked Günther's foot aside.

Günther held him. "You can't go now!"

"Yes, I can, I can!" the little boy screeched. He pushed Günther to the ground.

The two wrestled and rolled over in the dark.

There was a crash.

The candles went out.

The door was ripped from its hinges.

Glass shattered.

Dust penetrated the cellar.

The flickering light of many fires lit up our cellar.

We coughed, rubbed our eyes. We took a long time getting ourselves together.

"Where's the little one?" Günther asked into the red-flickering darkness.

He had disappeared.

"Everyone outside!" The order echoed through the cellar. "Bring your tools! Everyone must help!"

There was an enormous mountain of rubble in front of our *Heim*. It was the house I had taken shelter in.

First of all, we all ran home.

"We'll meet again at the *Heim!*" Günther called after me.

The Attack

The dust of ruins hung over every street. Whole blocks of houses had been razed to the ground. Flames many feet high shot up from the heaps of rubble. Men, women, and children were clambering among the ruins. Many were screaming. No one paid any attention to the ongoing air raid; everyone disregarded the falling red-hot fragments.

An old man ripped the spade out of my hand. "I need it more than you!" And he fell upon a heap of ruins and began to dig as if he were demented.

In our house the window panes were missing, but there was no other damage.

I turned back at once.

Men were already working opposite the *Heim*. "There are some people buried here!" one said. "We heard knocking. Come and help us!"

A little later Günther also returned. "Everything's okay!" he told me. "Only the roof's burned away." Then he, too, helped.

We began to clear away stones and bricks. There were no tools. We worked with our bare hands. We threw the small pieces, rolled the larger ones to the side; pieces too big to handle we bypassed altogether.

None of the others in our platoon had returned.

Gradually the air attack diminished. The droning stopped, the antiaircraft guns fell silent. Only the searchlights continued to sweep the sky until they, too, were turned off one after the other. The all-clear signal followed.

The sky above our town turned a fiery red after the dust had dispersed.

It began to grow light.

About an hour later a woman brought us a pickax. Now the men took turns splitting the large stones into portable pieces.

Günther and I hauled the pieces to a pile at the edge of the street.

Again and again we interrupted our work to listen for the knocks below. Then we'd lie on our stomachs, shape our hands into funnels, and shout into the rubble. "Hang on! We're on our way!"

Gradually other men and women joined us. Even an old woman loosened stones from the debris with shaking hands.

Meanwhile it had grown light. A beautiful blue sky streaked with smoke-gray clouds gleamed above us.

My hands hurt. My eyes smarted.

The men were digging with the ax handle outside the cellar entrance. A hand appeared, bloody from digging through the rubble.

A moment later we saw a second hand.

The man carefully shoveled out the arms.

Men gripped the arms and pulled.

Dirt slithered after them.

We enlarged the hole.

Again the men pulled.

A dusty gray face. Closed eyes. Abrasions on the cheeks. Deeper.

A torso in unrecognizable, shredded clothing. Deeper.

Below the knees smashed legs, feet crushed to a bloody, dust-encrusted mass.

"He's dead," the man said.

They laid him on top of the ruin.

Günther walked over to the body and wiped the dust from the face. Then he turned to me and said: "It's Otto!"

"Carry on!" the man ordered.

The Transfer

The building was in the center of a small park. It was generally known as the "Jew castle." Only the six-cornered star in the tracery above the entrance still reminded one of the former owner, and it was more than half covered by a sign that announced that this was now the Regional Office of the Hitler Youth.

We climbed the wide, carved wooden staircase to the second floor. We knocked on the door that bore the lettering: ANTEROOM OF THE REGIONAL LEADER.

Inside a girl leader in a brown combat jacket sat at a large desk. She looked up, quietly returned our greeting, and looked at us expectantly.

We both pulled letters from our pockets and handed them to her.

Günther explained, "We have been ordered to see the regional leader."

She took the letters from us and examined them at length.

"We would like to know. . . ." Günther began.

"The *Bannführer* will tell you in person," she cut him off in a friendly but firm manner. Then she invited us to sit down, adding: "The *Bannführer* is seeing visitors at the moment. I hope he won't be very long." And without paying us any further attention she turned back to her work.

We sat side by side by the window.

It was very quiet in the dark, wood-paneled room with the high ceiling. Only faintly did voices drift through the double doors leading to the regional leader's office. Over the desk beside the door hung a vast picture of the Führer. In field grays, Hitler looked down at us, imperious and stern.

Suddenly the handle on one of the doors was pressed down.

The girl leader jumped up at once and stood at attention, motioning us to do the same.

One of the two doors opened partway. We could hear a voice saying quite clearly: "By the first of the month I will expect your detailed and informative report on the means you have employed to improve recruitment of volunteers."

"Yes, sir!" a different voice replied.

The door flew open. Out came two men in brown uniforms, followed by our regional leader.

The Transfer

We saluted.

They nodded to the girl leader, ignored us.

Our *Bannführer* accompanied the two men to the out-side door. When he went to open it, his artificial right hand, covered with a brown glove, banged audibly against the wood paneling.

"Wasn't one—our state leader?" Günther asked softly.

"And the other was a staff leader from the Reich Youth Office," confirmed the girl. She sighed. "V.I.P.'s always bring unpleasant news."

The *Bannführer* was coming back. He looked at us. "Why are you here?" he asked.

"Because of the boy who disappeared," the girl replied on our behalf.

Günther's eyes widened in fright.

With his artificial hand the *Bannführer* pushed us into his office. At a sign from him, the girl followed with pad and pencil. At first he stood silently in front of us. Then he began to stride back and forth. While his right hand swung stiffly to and fro, his left played nervously with the Iron Cross, First Class, and the gold stripes he had received for his war injury. "A stupid thing!" he mumbled. "A really stupid thing!" Suddenly he stopped in front of us and addressed Günther. "I have to file a report on it! How could it have happened?"

And Günther told how the little boy had run from the air-raid shelter in a panic.

The girl in the corner took it all down.

When Günther had told him everything, the regional

leader turned to me. "You were there. You can testify to what he said?"

"Yes, sir!"

He resumed his pacing. "You know the boy hasn't been seen since. Nothing was found, no body, not so much as a shred of clothing. A stupid thing to have happened." He stopped and turned to look at Günther. "And he was your responsibility."

Günther pressed his lips tightly together.

"No stain from this incident must remain on the Hitler Youth. So what to do?" Our *Bannführer* thought for a moment. "How old are you?" he asked Günther abruptly.

"Sixteen," Günther answered.

"A pity, too young!" the *Bannführer* said. "Otherwise I'd have advised you to volunteer and everything would have been solved."

He continued his pacing.

Günther's hands shook; he looked wretched.

"I am sorry," the regional leader began afresh, "but I cannot keep you on as platoon leader."

The *Bannführer* laid his left hand on Günther's shoulder. "Don't worry! I will transfer you to another platoon until this matter has been forgotten."

Changes

When I got home, Father was standing in the kitchen. He returned my greeting sullenly. "Where've you been?" he asked.

"On duty!" I replied.

"Mother's standing in line at the grocer's," he said. "They got a shipment of real coffee."

I looked through the breadbox but couldn't find any bread.

"Hands off!" Father snapped at me. "We're hungry, too. Wait until mealtime, then we can divide things fairly. Everyone gets what he's due according to his ration cards!"

Discontented, I sat down at the table.

Father turned his back to me. He was working on the wire glass he had inserted into the window frames to replace the missing glass. After a while he asked: "What's the matter with Günther?"

I told him about Günther's transfer.

"And who's his successor?"

"A stranger from another group."

Father muttered to himself. There was a short silence, then he began afresh: "And you? Why didn't you become the new platoon leader?"

"I don't know!"

"Didn't you try for it?"

"I would have liked to be promoted," I admitted, "but they didn't pick me."

Father turned toward me. "What kind of boy are you?" he asked, disappointed. "How long have you been a member of the *Jungvolk* and the Hitler Youth? And what's become of you? Heinz! No effort required on his part. He was older than you and his father had a position in the Party. But even Günther, the son of that—well, whatever —he made it to platoon leader! I'm in the Party. And my son? I don't understand it!"

I sat at the table and couldn't think of an answer.

There was an enormous crater in the middle of the street. Huge heaps of rubble lined the road on both sides. For many hundreds of meters they blocked the way.

In a continuous chain about thirty Russian prisoners-of-war were hauling large and small blocks of stone to fill the hole. Exhausted, they stumbled up and down their path.

"In two hours' time traffic will flow through here again!" Günther's father announced. A rifle slung around him, he stood at the side of the road, rolled a cigarette, and watched the prisoners at work. From time to time he called to them a long drawn-out: "*Davai! Davai!*"

"What does *davai* mean?" I inquired.

"It means 'faster'!" he explained. "But it's not only for the Russians that I say it."

"They can't work any faster anyway," I said. "They look as if they might drop dead from starvation at any moment."

"They do sometimes," he told me. "But then they don't get anything but cabbage soup. Cabbage soup day in day out. . . ." He stubbed out his half-smoked cigarette and threw it away in the direction of the bomb crater.

At once two prisoners dropped the stones they were carrying and threw themselves onto the butt.

Günther's father turned his head away while they wrestled for it. "Poor devils!" he said.

"But we don't have enough either!" I put forward.

He looked at me.

"Well, should the prisoners live better than us?" I protested.

Günther's father took a deep breath. "God have mercy on us if we should lose this war," he said in a low voice. "If they ask us to account for everything we have done to them, then. . . . I don't dare to think it through."

I looked at the faces of the Russians: dull, without expression.

"We mustn't lose this war!" Günther's father said once more in a hard voice. "Not at any price. If they'd take me, I'd go to the front again! We must win !"

"Have you told Günther this?"

"If Günther wants to volunteer like your friend Heinz, I won't hinder him. Out there he can serve his fatherland better than he can here—every night in an air-raid shelter. And at least he'd wear a uniform he could be proud of."

"But you were always against war," I reminded him.

"War, boy, war," he repeated. "For me it hasn't been a question of war or Hitler for a long time now! For me it's only a matter of Germany now! If we lose this war, we lose Germany. And that's why we must be victorious!"

The car braked close beside us. The back door opened,

and Heinz's father called to us: "Come on, you two, get in. Quickly!"

We climbed into the car, Günther first. We said hello but had no chance to talk further because the radio beside the driver was broadcasting the military dispatch and we had to listen to it.

The conversation didn't really begin until we reached Heinz's father's study. He pushed us into soft upholstered armchairs and took three small glasses out of the side compartment of his bookcase. He pulled a bottle from behind the books and showed it to us. "Real French cognac!" he told us. "Something special, for special occasions only!" He uncorked it, filled the three glasses, and stood still. He raised his glass.

We worked ourselves out of the armchairs and picked up our glasses, too.

"I received notification early tonight that Heinz has been promoted to second lieutenant. You are his friends. Let's drink to his health!" And he emptied his glass in one gulp.

We did likewise. Then we congratulated him.

When we had sat down again, Heinz's father asked what we had been doing. Later he told us about Heinz. In the beginning there were funny stories, but they kept growing progressively more serious. Finally he remembered: "Now Heinz will be sent back to the front."

After a moment's silence he went on: "Pity you three couldn't stay together! You could have watched over each other. You know my boy, you know what he's like. When he does something, he does it wholeheartedly. He needs someone to watch over him. . . ." He poured us all another drink.

Wistfully, in almost a whisper, Heinz's father said: "I wish I could be with him; he is my only son!" His eyes shimmered in the light.

We got up. Heinz's father cleared his throat and accompanied us to the door. When he shook our hands to say good-bye, he declared: "I'll see to it that you two get evacuated to a camp in the country. You'll avoid the air raids and get enough sleep for once."

The Camp in the Country

We sat by the light of one dim bulb. Before each of us lay a mountain of socks. Gray and blue socks, some with holes too large for the darning egg, others so thin we didn't know if they were worth the yarn. We darned socks. We had been darning socks for three evenings in a row—and the piles didn't grow smaller.

"I tried the 'Faith and Beauty' outfit today," Günther was telling me. "They said they couldn't help. The leader has no time. Her girls have no time. They are all working in the war effort, they told me, and are so exhausted when they get back from the munitions factory they can barely mend their own things. So they can't possibly take on the socks of thirty boys."

"How will we manage?" I asked. "Until we've taught those ten-year-olds how to darn, they'll be running around barefoot. And we can't sit here every evening until far into the night darning socks. When and where can we prepare for day duty?"

Günther looked up from his work. "Tomorrow morning I'll try the village church choir once more. Perhaps they'll help us?!" He said nothing for a while. "If only the camp-director would help. But no! He leaves everything to his group leaders."

I felt so tired I had to be careful not to fall asleep over the darning.

In the dormitory next door things had still not quieted down.

"At home the children didn't sleep because of bombing raids," I said. "And here they don't sleep because they're homesick."

Günther had trouble staying awake. We out-yawned each other.

He bit off a wool thread and added the sock to the finished pile. "D'you know," he told me, "I have this 'evacuation to the country' bit up to here. So you sit in the country and can't do a thing except look after children during the day and darn socks at night. It's so utterly absurd! I wish I could volunteer like Heinz." He had just picked up another pair of socks when there was a knock on the door.

"Come in!" called Günther.

The door was opened hesitantly.

In came one of the boys from the dormitory. His white nightshirt reached down to his feet. His hair stood on end. He squinted against the brightness, then saluted with raised hand: "Heil Hitler, Group Leaders!"

Casually Günther responded: "Heil Hitler!"

I, too, mumbled the greeting.

"What's going on?" Günther inquired. "Why are you up in the middle of the night?"

The boy hesitated, then replied: "I only wanted to report that Paul is gone."

Günther and I leaped to our feet.

Günther had turned pale; his mouth was agape. Nervously he asked: "Gone where?"

The boy shrugged. "I don't know."

Günther flung aside the socks he had been about to darn. "How long has Paul been gone?"

"A long time."

"Why didn't you let us know before?"

"Paul didn't want me to," the boy confessed. "And I thought he'd come back by himself."

When the light in the dormitory came on, even those already asleep woke up at once.

Günther walked across to the foot of Paul's bed. It looked as if Paul was hidden beneath the blankets. He had created that impression with a nightshirt and a bundle of old newspapers. The bed felt cold to the touch. Otherwise there was nothing to discover.

Günther ran to Paul's locker.

The locker stood open. The knapsack was missing. Only three or four pieces of underwear still lay in the compartments. Dirty laundry was crumpled up in the bottom of the locker.

"Boys," Günther began, "you must help me. Paul has disappeared. Does anyone know where he's gone?"

An arm was raised in one corner. "He always said he wanted to go home to his mother."

"Does Paul have any money?"

"He borrowed one mark from me. He was going to return it by mail when he got home."

"I lent him fifty pfennigs."

"How was Paul going to get home?" Günther asked.

"On foot and hitchhiking."

"Does he know the way?"

"He was going to follow the river until he came to the nearest bridge. Street signs begin there."

"Then he'll run right into the marsh!" shouted Günther. "Does anyone else know anything important? I must go right after him!"

The boys thought. "He saved a whole sandwich for the road," one said.

Günther thought of something else. "What's Paul wearing?"

"Shorts and brown shirt!" the boys declared.

"Well, boys," Günther concluded, "please stay quiet. I'll find Paul and bring him back!"

We turned out the light and left the dormtiory. The boys behind us were uncannily quiet.

"It takes about an hour to get to the marsh," Günther

estimated. "So Paul's already there! Perhaps—" He looked at me.

I contradicted him. "He wouldn't use the road. If he's gone along the river, he'll take longer."

We were wide awake.

"Useless!" Günther groaned. "How can I catch up with him?"

Thoughts chased each other—but I couldn't think of anything.

"No car going in that direction this time of night!" I said.

Günther paced up and down without stopping.

"The camp director's bicycle!" I suddenly thought.

Günther raced off at once. I ran after him. We pounded on the director's door. No reply.

We rattled the handle. No one opened.

"Off again!" Günther ground his teeth. "Isn't there anyone here who can help?" he groaned.

We went down the stairs. The bicycle stood in the shed. It was chained to a post.

"What now?" Günther asked, discouraged.

"We must inform the police right away!" I reminded him.

Günther refused. "Until they start searching, it'll be too late. The search must start at once."

I regarded the bicycle. "Then we'll have to smash the chain."

Finally we managed to break the chain. The bike ended up minus three spokes and with a bent fork—but it still ran.

Günther swung himself aboard. "Wait a while before you call the police. Look after the children!"

He pedaled off standing up and didn't look back.

When I entered the dormitory, the boys were talking among themselves. I turned on the light and sat down on Paul's bed. They went right on exchanging advice on how to behave in a marsh.

Others sat on their beds, lost in thought.

One boy suddenly said: "Paul's father was killed in action. He has no brothers or sisters. His mother's all alone at home. That's why he wanted to get home."

"Will Paul's father be buried here or at home?" another inquired.

I tried to get them to talk about something else, but didn't succeed. All our thoughts circled around Paul.

"I don't want to die all alone," Paul's bed neighbor whispered.

The door to the dormitory burst open.

The boys looked up.

In the doorway stood the camp director. "What's going on here?" he bellowed. "What do you think you are doing?"

I got up to report what had happened.

But he wouldn't let me speak. "Having a cozy chat in the middle of the night, eh? Must have been bored, right?" He turned to me. "So you sit up with the children and keep them from getting to sleep!" He was screaming and his breath smelled of alcohol. "Where's Günther?"

I finally managed to explain. I also told him about the bicycle.

Instead of answering he dashed out of the room. He returned with the torn chain in his hand. He was raving. And the more he raged, the angrier he became.

The boys huddled in their beds, watching the screeching camp director and me. "Have the police been here yet?" he wanted to know.

I told him the truth.

He grew still at once. Almost in a whisper he said: "You didn't report the runaway to the police right away? And you call yourself a group leader?" He turned and disappeared.

About an hour later two policemen appeared. They had me and then the boys tell them everything all over again. They wrote down what struck them as important. Then they seized the things in Paul's locker.

The camp director kept pointing out that Günther and I had broken his bicycle chain. They noted that down on their pads as well. After that they paid no more attention to me. When they said good-bye to the camp director, they told him they'd put through a tracer in the morning.

We were all standing in the dormitory.

One policeman turned to the boys and said, "I hope none of you has the bright idea to run away. He'll be sorry, I swear it!"

At that moment Günther pushed a grubby and weeping Paul into the room.

"I will arrange for your immediate recall!" the camp

director snapped at Günther. "Incapable of looking after a few children!"

The Physical

"So you've finished reading all those cowboys-and-Indian stories," the army physician with the face full of dueling scars was saying, "and now you want to experience real adventures so you've volunteered for military service."

Naked and shivering, we stood lined up against the wall and said nothing in reply.

A sergeant major weighing at least two hundred pounds measured us, examined our eyes, and tested our hearing.

"A plague must have broken out among the Hitler boys," the physician began again. "And apparently there's only one cure against it: the Iron Cross, First Class. Well, it's okay by me!"

The sergeant major led us to the desk. The physician pushed his glasses up on his forehead and eyed us from top to bottom. "You may be usable as skeletons," he decided, "but you still have to become men." He tapped and listened. "About face!"

We turned around.

"Which branch?" he asked.

"Infantry!" Günther and I answered simultaneously.

"What?" The army physician straightened up and stared at us. "Well, I guess you're always good enough for the infantry." All at once he spoke emphatically: "You know you can pick the service you want as volunteers—always assuming I declare you fit, of course."

"Yes, sir!"

"And you still want to go to the infantry? Not the air force? Or the navy?"

"Yes, sir!"

"Did they inject you with hero mania in the Hitler Youth?"

We couldn't think of an answer.

"Any other wishes?" he asked.

"Yes, sir!" Günther replied. "We would both like to be assigned to the same unit."

"Same domicile, same service branch, same reserve unit," growled the fat sergeant major in the background.

The physician bent over his desk. "Put on your uniforms, go home, and each of you get hold of a cardboard box. I'll see what I can do for you."

XI

-1943-

Night

We stood by the railroad tracks and waited. Our packs lay at our feet. A cold wind made us shiver. There were woods as far as we could see: birch trees and fir trees. The tracks came out of a cutting and disappeared into another. The only building anywhere in sight was a kind of signal box made of thick wooden planks, with embrasures instead of windows and an earthworks around it. We could follow the telephone trunk line from an embrasure to where it disappeared in a clump of trees.

The first lieutenant who had brought us here marched back and forth in front of us. He kept looking at the sky and rubbing his hands. From time to time he'd cup his ears and listen in the direction of the woods.

Night

Time passed.

All of a sudden a master sergeant and another noncommissioned officer appeared. No one had heard or seen them approach.

The master sergeant took over the command from the lieutenant.

"Reinforcements, fresh from the Hitler Youth!" the lieutenant told him. He immediately disappeared into the blocklike hut.

The master sergeant inspected us one after the other, then he ordered us to pick up our packs and weapons and follow him in single file.

The other noncommissioned officer brought up the rear.

Indifferently we trotted through the pathless woods. The underbrush afforded hardly a glimpse on either side. The ground gurgled beneath each step, and our footprints immediately filled with reddish-brown water.

Günther turned around. "My boots are full of water," he said.

I had wet feet, too.

It took us about an hour and a half to cross the woods. We saw nothing but stunted trees and under the trees puddles of water. We heard nothing but the squishing and gurgling of the ground, and from time to time a whispered word.

All at once we found ourselves at the edge of a clearing. We could make out squat wooden buildings crouched among the trees on the other side: bunkers. Smoke came from short chimneys. A dog jumped toward us, barking.

We stopped, closed up ranks. We stood in the middle

of the clearing and sank deeper into the ground by the moment.

Across the corduroy road which led from bunker to bunker, a colonel was approaching. He wore a dirty camouflage jacket. He greeted us briefly and explained that we would be divided among the units. Then he hurried back to his bunker in large steps.

From somewhere far away came the muffled sound of gunfire.

We flinched.

A shell howled over our heads.

We cowered. The soggy ground was not welcoming.

Unmoved, the master sergeant collected our papers.

The shell exploded in the woods not far away.

Again a volley, again the howling, again the impact.

After the third strike, only a few still kept their eyes closed.

The master sergeant made us count off.

I changed over to Günther's rank. Soon it would be our turn. Five ranks to go, four—at last we were assigned.

A young officer was talking to two already assigned ranks. His back was turned to us.

"Sir!" Günther suddenly shouted across the clearing.

The master sergeant looked up from his lists. "What do you think you're doing? Have you gone crazy?"

The second lieutenant had turned around and was coming closer. His eyes were searching for the caller.

Günther snapped to attention, clicked his heels so water sprayed high.

"Günther!" the lieutenant called out. He rushed toward us. He embraced Günther. Then he saw me as well. He slapped my shoulder so hard my rifle fell into the mud. "You're both here! That's unbelievable!"

He pulled us out of the rank and swung us around in front of everybody.

The master sergeant stood there with a stupid look on his face. Heinz stopped right in front of him. "These two are mine," he said.

"Impossible, sir!" said the master sergeant. "They've already been assigned to another unit."

"Then exchange them!"

"But sir, the lists have already been made up."

"Well, change them!" Heinz ordered. He held both our shoulders and pushed us across the clearing to the men he had already accepted.

"Sir, what shall I report to the other unit if you take two extra men?"

"My best regards, and that I need these two!"

It was terribly dark.

Everybody held onto the pack of the man in front of him. In that way we tried to find our way across the soggy forest ground as noiselessly as possible.

Ahead of us a machine gun was slowly firing. From time to time a single shot fell. Suddenly a white Very light hung in the sky above us, spreading a chalky light over the crippled birches. Its reflection was mirrored a thousandfold in the marshy puddles around us.

We did not move until the Very light had burned itself out.

Then we walked on, still blinded by the light.

I lost the man in front of me. I took two hurried steps to catch up with him, slipped, and sat in a water-filled hole. The water came up to my gun belt. I screamed.

"Quiet!" a voice snapped on my left. Footsteps approached. A hand pulled me up. "Pay attention! Hold on to the man in front of you!" the same voice grumbled. My hand was placed on someone's backpack.

A moment later the column marched on. Silently and blindly we tapped our way across the slippery ground. The sounds of gunfire came closer, and closer.

My wet pants clung to my legs, cold as ice. I was cold. And tired, so very tired. Sometimes I saw veiled figures dancing in front of my eyes. Branches struck my face. Sometimes they hit my steel helmet with a muffled sound.

Whenever this happened, the same order was passed down from the front: "Quiet! No noise!"

Suddenly we stopped, in the middle of the woods.

I walked into a wall of thick tree trunks.

Something creaked.

Another Very light went up.

We stood like statues.

I could now make out a very high wall made of tree trunks. I saw we were all leaning against a wooden bunker, one beside the other.

The Very light burned itself out.

A machine gun barked—three, four times.

Night

I was thrust against the wooden wall. It gave way. I stumbled, got entangled in a hanging blanket, and pitched into a narrow room that was lit by a single candle.

"Some ass pulled down our blanket!" a voice complained.

I wanted to ask what was happening when there was an explosion close to the bunker. It was repeated three, four times.

"Mortars!"

I stood up. Around me, squeezed into the narrow bunker, were all the others from my reserve unit.

Günther was pushing his helmet to the back of his head.

Heinz was there, too. He was talking to a corporal who was lying on a cot.

An old sergeant was sitting at a roughly hewn table, guarding the little candle flame from any drafts.

The corporal climbed off his cot, and another corporal joined him.

"Three for the first platoon and three for the third!" Heinz ordered.

The six disappeared with the two corporals.

"You two stay here!" Heinz told Günther and me. "It's now 23:00 hours. Find a cot and sleep. You go on guard duty from three to six."

I looked around.

Multi-decker bunks stood against every wall of the bunker. Enlisted men lay asleep in most of them, but in one corner slept a staff sergeant.

I flung my pack onto a bottom bunk.

The soldier in the bunk above opened his eyes. "Get off!" he growled. "That's the lieutenant's cot."

I finally found an empty top bunk. It was one of three and so close to the ceiling you had to roll yourself in and out of it.

Heinz was bent over a map on the table beside the sergeant.

"You really mean to use the new ones tonight?" the old sergeant asked softly.

"Of course!" Heinz answered. "It's the perfect opportunity. It frees experienced people to come with us, and the new ones can't do any harm because they won't have permission to fire!"

"Whatever you say, sir!"

"I'll just go across to the command post," Heinz said. He lifted the blanket and left the bunker.

I had begun to pull off my wet pants.

"What on earth are you doing?" the sergeant inquired in astonishment.

"I want to hang up my pants to dry."

"You sure you don't have a screw loose? You can't take your pants off in here!"

"But they're dripping wet!" I replied.

"And if the comrades from the other side should arrive," laughed the sergeant, "you'll just receive them in your underpants? They'll be delighted."

I still held the pants in my hands.

"Get on with it!" he ordered. "Put your pants and boots on at once, and lie down!"

Night

I obeyed and climbed into my bunk. Though I wrapped the blanket around me tightly, I shivered with cold and couldn't fall asleep.

Heinz came back. "Everything's arranged. There'll be no firing in our section from three to seven-thirty A.M. The two neighboring sections will provide diverting fire. At three the new guards will take over. At three-fifteen I will start out with you and five other men. The path through the minefield is marked."

Heinz talked on.

And I fell asleep after all.

It was about four o'clock.

Günther and I stood in a small box made of logs. It was so small you could barely turn around. We stared through the firing port into the gray nothingness in front of us. My pants clung wetly to my calves. I was cold. My lids kept trying to close. My head kept sinking to my chest. But again and again I pulled myself upright.

Günther, too, was dozing. His chin was propped on the butt of his machine gun.

Our section lay deathly still. But to our right and left bursts of fire tore the quiet in irregular intervals: short bursts of machine gun fire; single rifle shots; at one time even three rounds of heavy shells.

Without making a sound the staff sergeant crept to our guard post from behind. "Listen closely!" he whispered. "Remember: you must not fire. Our people are ahead. You can shoot only if you recognize an attack."

"What's going on then?" asked Günther.

"The general staff needs a prisoner from the other side. And we have been elected to get him. A mission for potential suicides. Pray for the lieutenant." He looked through our embrasure. When he turned he saw our faces. "Aren't you the two the lieutenant knows?" he asked.

"We were with him in the *Jungvolk* and the Hitler Youth."

"Oh yes, the Hitler Youth—a generation of heroes!" he said mockingly. And a while later: "But our lieutenant is a fine man. Ought to have more like him! He needs someone to look after him, though."

Before he left he warned us once more: "Don't fall asleep! And don't fire unless you are attacked!" Then he went on his way to the next guard post.

Again it was quiet around us. On the other side nothing moved either. Only rarely did we hear a shot or the bark of a machine gun. Soon fatigue overcame me once more. Wisps of fog before our lookout thickened into ghosts, dissolved, weaved, and I began to be afraid. Each time I opened my eyes I started. I was sure I saw an attacker in front of our post. Uncanny! I looked across at Günther.

Günther had his eyes closed.

I nudged him.

Günther jumped, jerked. The burst of fire tore through the quiet in our section.

I smashed the machine gun from Günther's hand.

For one short moment everything remained still, deadly still.

Then flares went up on the other side.

Three, four machine guns began to hammer almost at the same time.

Mortars barked.

Rifle shots cracked.

Artillery pounded.

Shells whined closer, crashed into the ground in front of our post.

Everything turned into an inferno: rumblings, roars, bursts, explosions. Colors went from chalky white to greenish blue, to screaming yellow and flaming red. The ground trembled, shook. Crashing, fizzing, hissing. We smelled fire, burning bodies. There were screams, whimpers, moans.

We huddled into ourselves.

Grenades hollowed out the earth.

Shells ripped branches to shreds.

Splinters slit up tree trunks.

Logs burned.

We ducked down.

Günther's teeth chattered. He moaned.

I was dreadfully afraid.

"My God!" moaned Günther. "Heinz!—*Heinz!*" he suddenly screamed. He jumped up, vaulted the fence, started running, flung himself into the inferno. "Heinz!" he yelled. "Heinz!"

Volley after volley rolled against our position, in an impenetrable barrage of steel and flames.

Notes

Page 1   *"Germany Awake!"*   The rallying cry of the Nazi organizations; after a song by Dietrich Eckart (1868–1923).

Page 3   *swastika.*   The hooked cross 卐 was the emblem of the Nazi party and, from 1935, the whole Third Reich. The German flag showed the black swastika in a white disk against a red background. (Adolf Hitler wrote in *Mein Kampf* [My Struggle]: "A symbol it really is! In *red* we see the social ideal of the movement, in *white* the nationalist idea, in the *swastika* the mission of the struggle for the victory of the Aryan man.")

Page 3

Hitler Youths. Members of the Nazi youth organization, into which all the youth in the Third Reich were organized. Originally the junior branch of the S.A. (see note for p. 7), the Hitler Youth was formed as one of the principal organizations of the Nazi party in 1935. Baldur von Schirach, as Reich Youth Leader, was responsible directly to Hitler. The Hitler Youth was a vast organization built on paramilitary lines resembling that of the S.A., with its own system of ranks and promotions, its own leadership schools and training camps. In 1936, membership in the Nazi youth organization became compulsory for all children from ages ten to eighteen.

Boys. Although a boy could not officially join the Hitler Youth until the age of ten, he served a kind of apprenticeship as a *Pimpf* from the age of six to ten. During that time a record was kept of his accomplishments in ideology, athletics, military science (i.e., putting up tents, map-reading, spying, recognizing trees, etc.), and Party activities. Upon graduation to the *Jungvolk* at age ten, he would wear a uniform usually consisting of heavy black shoes, black shorts, brown shirt and swastika armband (*and* dagger), and continue his training, including hiking trips, war games, etc. At the age of fourteen he would become a member of the Hitler Youth proper, where his training became strictly military in orientation, with heavy emphasis on rifle drill, military information, knowledge and use of explosives, etc. Uniforms were brown with red swastika armbands, though some winter uniforms were dark blue. A boy stayed in the Hitler Youth until the age of eighteen, when he passed into the Labor Service and/or military service.

Girls. Like boys, girls were organized into youth groups—*Jungmädel* (Young Maidens) for girls under fourteen, and the *Bund Deutscher Mädel* (League of German Maidens) for ages fourteen to eighteen. At eighteen, all girls did a year's service on farms or in munition factories—their equivalent to the Labor Service of the young men. Although training in the girls' groups was similar to that of the boys', there was less emphasis on military prowess and more emphasis on their role in the Third Reich—to become mothers of healthy children. Their uniforms consisted of heavy marching shoes, full blue skirts, white blouses, and cotton neckerchiefs with wooden rings bearing the group insignia. Heavy blue "training suits" were worn in bad weather.

An approximate breakdown of the organization of the Hitler Youth is on page 184.

HITLER YOUTH ORGANIZATIONS

AGES 10—14		AGES 14—18		EXPLANATION
Boys	Girls	Boys	Girls	
Jungvolk (Young Folk)	Jungmädel (Young Maidens)	Hitlerjugend (Hitler Youth)	Bund Deutscher Mädel (League of German Maidens)	Title of Organization
Reichsjugendführer*	Reichsjugendführer	Reichsjugendführer	Reichsjugendführer	Reich Youth Leader (B. von Schirach)
Jungbann (sometimes called Oberjungstamm)	Jungmädeluntergau	Bann	Untergau	highest regional subdivision: approx. 3000–3600 people
Jungstamm	Jungmädelring	Stamm	Mädelring	2nd largest subdivision: approx. 500–600 people
Fähnlein	Jungmädelgruppe	Gefolgschaft	Mädelgruppe	detachment of approx. 100–150 people
Jungzug	Jungmädelschar	Schar	Mädelschar	equivalent of a platoon: approx. 30–45 people
Jungenschaft	Jungmädelschaft	Kameradschaft	Mädelschaft	squad of approx. 10–15 people

* N.B. The leaders of the various detachments were named simply by adding the word "führer" after the name of the particular group, i.e. *Fähnleinführer, Jungstammführer,* or "führerin" in the case of girls.

Notes

Page 4   *Hitler.* Adolf Hitler (1889–1945) maneuvered toward obtaining the chancellorship of Germany and he succeeded on January 30, 1933. Hitler was often referred to simply as the Führer (the Leader), a title that was never used by itself except when referring to him.

Page 4   Ernst *Thaelmann* (1886–1944) was the leader of the Communist Party in Germany.

Page 4   *brown.* Color of uniforms worn by S.A. men (see *storm troopers*).

Page 7   *storm troopers.* Members of the S.A., abbreviation of *Sturm Abteilungen,* which literally means "Assault Sections." Often referred to simply as "Brown Shirts."

Page 8   *Song.* "When the golden evening sun." A favorite song of the Nazis, by Karl H. Muschalla.

Page 9   *Heil Hitler!* (Hail Hitler!) The prescribed stiff-arm salute at eye level. "Sieg Heil!" (Hail to victory!) was also acceptable.

Page 10   *Song:* "In the German land we march." This song by Herbert Hammer was originally called "In *Great Berlin* we march." The "Red brood" refers to members of the Communist Party.

Page 13   *Song:* "Raise high the flags." Also referred to as the *Horst Wessel Lied* because it was written by the S.A. leader, Horst Wessel (1907–1930). It was later elevated to the status of a second national anthem.

I WAS THERE

Page 15   *Equality*.   The request for equality was aimed at the provision of the Treaty of Versailles (signed by Germany June 28, 1919), which limited Germany to a hundred-thousand-man army.

                   Right to Self-Determination. Another reference to Hitler's determination to rid Germany of the "shackles" imposed on it by the Allied victors after World War I.

Page 15   *Field Marshal von Hindenburg*. President of Germany from 1925 to his death on August 2, 1934. On that date Hitler became absolute dictator of Germany.

Page 16   *Pimpf*. A kind of apprentice for the Hitler Youth (see note for p. 3, *Hitler Youths*).

Page 18   *Nationalsozialistische Deutsche Arbeiter Partei*. Full title of the Nazi party. "Nazi" is derived from "*Nat*ionalso*zi*alistische Deutsche Arbeiter Partei" (NSDAP)—the National Socialist German Workers' Party, of which Adolf Hitler was the "Supreme Leader."

Page 20   *victory rune*. Emblem of the *Jungvolk* in the shape of a bolt of lightning, derived from the Germanic runic alphabet.

                   Song: "When we march side by side." A song of the pre-Hitler German youth movement that was officially adopted by the Hitler Youth. Text: Hermann Claudius; Melody: Armin Knab.

Notes

Page 27   *black uniforms*. In contrast to the brown-shirted S.A. men, the members of the infamous S.S. (⚡⚡) or *Schutzstaffel* (lit., protection or guard detachment) wore black uniforms. Formed in 1925, the S.S. under Himmler became the most powerful (and feared) paramilitary organization within the Nazi party—a state within the State.

Page 28   *Winterhilfswerk*. This Winter Relief Fund was "established [in September, 1933] by the Nazis for the relief of the unemployed, to which all were exhorted to contribute generously. Apart from cheques sent as a result of blackmail or as 'insurance,' public collections were made at street corners and from door to door, often with threats and menaces." (J. W. Wheeler-Bennett: *Nemesis of Power,* Macmillan, London, 1964) Later, most of the moneys collected ended up in State coffers.

Page 39   *Treaty of Versailles*. The terms of the Versailles Treaty, laid down by the victorious Allies after World War I, restored Alsace-Lorraine to France, a parcel of territory to Belgium, a similar parcel in Schleswig to Denmark, and gave back to the Poles the lands which the Germans had taken during the partition of Poland. The Treaty of Versailles also required Germany to make reparation payments and virtually disarmed it.

I WAS THERE

everyone was supposed to eat a one-dish meal and contribute the money thus saved to the Winter Relief Fund (see *Winterhilfswerk*). The amounts were collected by Party officials and carefully recorded.

Page 82   *Kraft durch Freude* (Strength Through Joy). This department of the German Labor Front was established in 1933 to provide cheap vacations and other recreational programs (i.e., theater visits, saving for a Volkswagen, etc.) for low-paid workers. The German Labor Front under Dr. Robert Ley was the largest affiliated organization of the NSDAP and comprised all guilds, corporations and professional organizations after the trade unions were forcibly dissolved.

Page 82   *Ostmark*. Name given to Austria during the period of its annexation to Germany (1938–1945).

Page 87   *Sudetenland*. Name of Sudeten German territory in Czechoslovakia.

Page 90   *cannons*. Hermann Göring (1893–1946), Hitler's economic dictator responsible for the implementation of the Four-Year Plan, in a speech asserted that Germans wanted "guns instead of butter." While iron was imported, Germans were asked to go without butter.

Page 92   *Crystal Night.* The name given the nation-wide pogrom that took place during the night of November 9–10, 1938. The name was suggestive of the plate glass shattered in the course of the pogrom, when 7,500 Jewish shops and 400 synagogues were destroyed.

Page 93   *Goebbels claims.* Joseph Goebbels (1897–1945), Hitler's propaganda minister, claimed the "Crystal Night" pogrom had consisted of "spontaneous demonstrations" against German Jews. In actual fact, he had *arranged* for them in retaliation for the murder of Ernst vom Rath, third secretary of the German Embassy in Paris, by the seventeen-year-old German Jewish refugee Herschel Grynszpan.

Page 98   *Gefolgschaftsführer.* Leader of a detachment of Hitler Youths (see *Hitler Youths*).

Page 100   *Song:* "Forward!" This song, written by the Reich Youth Leader, Baldur von Schirach, was *the* song of the Hitler Youth.

Page 105   *Siegfried Line (Westwall).* A heavily fortified line built by the Germans along the French and Belgian border.

Page 109   *Stuka.* Abbreviated form of *Sturzkampf-bomber,* the feared German bomber plane of World War II, which dropped its bombs while diving toward its target and making a terrifying howling sound.

Page 110   *Iron Cross, First Class.* Highest German military decoration of World War II.

Page 113   *The Hitler Boy Quex* by Karl Aloys described the fate of a Hitler boy before 1933, who was murdered by Communists. P. C. E. Highofer's *Ghosts at the Dead Man* was a war book about the battle of Verdun in World War I, glorifying the soldier's role.

     The Wanderer Between Two Worlds by Walter Flex was a popular young people's book predating Hitler, and Hans Grimm's *Folk Without Space* incorporated Hitler's demand for more "living space" for Germany in a dramatic story.

Page 124   *cord.* The color of the cord indicated the rank of leaders in the Hitler youth organizations.

Page 124   *Song:* "A young folk stands ready." A popular song by Werner Altendorf.

Page 130   *harvest duty.* Part of Labor Service, compulsory.

Page 133   *silver braiding.* Indicated the rank of a staff sergeant.

I WAS THERE

Chronology
-1933-

January 30, 1933	Adolf Hitler becomes Chancellor of the German Reich.
February 27, 1933	The Reichstag (German parliament) building in Berlin burns down.
February 28, 1933	Hitler persuades President Hindenburg to sign a decree "for the Protection of People and State," which lays the foundation for a National Socialist dictatorship. Described as a "defensive measure against Communist acts of violence endangering the State," the decree suspended the seven sections of the German

constitution which guaranteed individual and civil liberties.

March 5, 1933

In the *Reichstagwahl* (parliamentary elections)—the last democratic elections during Hitler's lifetime—the NSDAP (Nationalsozialistische Deutsche Arbeiter Partei = National Socialist German Workers' [Nazi] Party) wins 288 of 648 seats. After the eighty-one Communist members of the *Reichstag* are forcibly excluded, the Nazi party has the majority.

March 24, 1933

The so-called "Enabling Act" takes all legislative power away from parliament and hands it over to Hitler's Government for four years. The act, which stipulates that Hitler may enact laws that "might deviate from the constitution," forms the legal basis for Hitler's dictatorship.

March, 1933

The first concentration camps are set up.

April 1, 1933

Hitler proclaims the first national boycott of Jewish stores.

May–July, 1933

Most political parties "voluntarily" dissolve themselves. On June 22 the Socialist Democrats are declared "subversive and inimical to the State" and outlawed.

July 14, 1933	A law decrees that "the National Socialist German Workers' Party constitutes the only political party in Germany."
September 9, 1933	The fifth annual convention of the Nazi party is celebrated in Nuremberg as the "Party Convention of Victory."
October 15, 1933	Germany leaves the League of Nations.
November 12, 1933	The NSDAP receives an overwhelming ninety-two percent on a one-party ballot.

-1934-

August 2, 1934	Reich President Paul von Hindenburg dies. Adolf Hitler becomes *Führer und Reichskanzler* (Leader and Reich Chancellor).
August 8, 1934	In a national plebiscite, ninety percent of the voters support Hitler as Führer and Reichskanzler.
September 4, 1934	Sixty thousand Hitler Youths parade at the sixth Nazi party congress in Nuremberg ("Triumph of Will").

-1935-

January 1, 1935	Ninety-one percent of the inhabitants of the Saar region vote for a return to the German Reich.
March 1, 1935	The Saar is formally returned to the German Reich.
March 16, 1935	Hitler reinstitutes compulsory military service in open defiance of the provisions of the Versailles Treaty.
September 10, 1935	"Reich Party Rally of Freedom" in Nuremberg. The swastika flag becomes the German national flag.
September 15, 1935	Proclamation of "Nuremberg Laws": Jews are deprived of German citizenship and reduced to the status of "subjects"; marriage and any sexual relations between Jews and Aryans are prohibited; Jews may no longer employ Aryan servants under the age of thirty-five.
October 3, 1935	Mussolini's Italian armies invade Abyssinia.

-1936-

March 7, 1936   German armed forces occupy the demilitarized Rhineland.

March 29, 1936   Hitler dissolves the Reichstag and calls for new "elections" and a referendum on his move into the Rhineland. Ninety-nine percent of the voters support Hitler's action.

August 1, 1936   The Olympic Games open in Berlin.

August 24, 1936   Two-year compulsory military service in the *Deutsche Wehrmacht* (German armed forces) is reintroduced.

October 25, 1936   Germany and Italy sign the so-called "Rome-Berlin Axis" protocol.

November 25, 1936   Germany and Japan sign the Anti-Comintern Pact.

December 1, 1936   Hitler's "Youth Law" makes membership in the Hitler Youth compulsory and outlaws all non-Nazi youth organizations.

-1937-

January 30, 1937	Hitler extends the "Enabling Act" for another four years.
July 7, 1937	Fighting breaks out between Chinese and Japanese troops near Peiping.
November 5, 1937	Hitler announces his war plans (Hossbach Protocol) to top advisers.

-1938-

February 4, 1938	Hitler names himself "Supreme Commander of the Armed Forces."
March 11–13, 1938	German troops march into Austria. Austria is annexed and becomes the *Ostmark*.
October 1, 1938	German troops "peacefully occupy" the Sudeten German territories in Czechoslovakia.
November 9–10, 1938	The "Crystal Night" pogrom takes place throughout Germany.
December 6, 1938	Germany and France sign a "nonaggression" pact.

-1939-

March 15, 1939	Hitler's troops march into Czechoslovakia. Czechoslovakia is incorporated into the Greater German Reich.
March 23, 1939	German troops "annex" Memel, a Baltic port of some four hundred thousand inhabitants, which had been lost to Lithuania after Versailles.
March 31, 1939	Neville Chamberlain, Prime Minister of Great Britain, makes the historic declaration in the House of Commons that Britain and France "would feel themselves bound at once to lend the Polish Government all support in their power" if Poland were attacked by Hitler's armies.
April 7, 1939	Italy occupies Albania.
May 22, 1939	Germany and Italy strengthen their military alliance with the "Pact of Steel."
August 23, 1939	The Nazi-Soviet nonaggression pact is signed in Moscow.
August 26, 1939	The first food ration cards are distributed.
September 1, 1939	Germany attacks Poland.

September 3, 1939	England and France declare war on Nazi Germany. *The Polish war becomes World War II.*
September 17, 1939	Soviet troops invade Poland.
October 1, 1939	The fighting in Poland stops.
October 6, 1939	Hitler proposes peace to England and France.
November 1, 1939	Germany annexes the German territories in Poland that it had lost through the Versailles Treaty.
November 7, 1939	Belgium and the Netherlands appeal jointly for peace and force a temporary postponement of Hitler's offensive against these two countries.
November 8, 1939	A bomb meant for Hitler explodes too late in the Munich Bürgerbräukeller.
November 30, 1939	Soviet troops attack Finland.

-1940-

March 12, 1940	Finland and Soviet Russia sign a peace treaty.

Chronology

April 9, 1940	German troops invade Denmark and Norway. Denmark surrenders.
May 10, 1940	The beginning of the Western campaign: Nazis invade the Netherlands, Belgium, and Luxembourg.
May 11, 1940	Chamberlain resigns and Winston Churchill takes office as Prime Minister of Great Britain. English bombers raid German targets for the first time.
May 12, 1940	German troops cross French frontiers.
May 14, 1940	Conquest of the Netherlands is completed.
May 18, 1940	Eupen-et-Malmédy and Moresnet are "returned" to the German Reich.
May 28, 1940	Belgium falls.
June 4, 1940	British troops evacuate Dunkirk.
June 8, 1940	Norway surrenders.
June 10, 1940	Italy enters the war and invades France.
June 14, 1940	German forces enter undefended Paris.
June 22, 1940	Truce with France.
July 10, 1940	The Battle of Britain begins.

September 6, 1940	The German *Luftwaffe* (air force) begins to pound English cities.
September 27, 1940	The German-Italian-Japanese Tripartite Pact is signed in Berlin.
October 28, 1940	Italian troops invade Greece.

-1941-

February 6, 1941	The famed *Afrika Korps* is formed under Field Marshal Rommel.
April 6, 1941	Start of the German campaign against Yugoslavia and Greece.
April 17, 1941	Successful end of the German campaign in Yugoslavia.
April 23, 1941	Greek forces capitulate.
May 18, 1941	The Italian forces in Abyssinia capitulate.
May 20, 1941	The battle for Crete begins.

June 22, 1941	Hitler attacks the Soviet Union.
September 23, 1941	The first test gassings of Jews take place in the Auschwitz camp.
December 6, 1941	German troops are halted in Russia.
December 7, 1941	Japan attacks Pearl Harbor.
December 8, 1941	Great Britain and the U.S. declare war on Japan.
December 11, 1941	Germany and Italy declare war on the U.S. The U.S. declares war on both those countries.

-1942-

January 20, 1942	Hitler decides on his "Final Solution" of the Jewish "problem" at the Wannsee conference.
March, 1942	The first large-scale RAF bombing raids on German cities take place.
June 28, 1942	New German offensive on the Eastern Front.

October, 1942	Nine-tenths of Stalingrad has fallen to German troops. German success in the east has reached its apex.
November 7, 1942	Allied troops land in North Africa.
November 11, 1942	German troops enter unoccupied parts of France.
November 22, 1942	Russian troops encircle Stalingrad, but Hitler orders the Sixth Army to stand firm.

-1943-

January 31– February 2, 1943	The remnants of the Sixth Army surrender to the Russians at Stalingrad, foreshadowing the collapse of Hitler's Third Reich more than two years later.

ABOUT THE AUTHOR

Hans Peter Richter is the author of over twenty books for young readers, including the highly acclaimed FRIEDRICH. First published in Germany, it has since appeared in England, Scotland, Spain, Denmark, Holland, Sweden and France, as well as in the United States. In 1972 FRIEDRICH was chosen for the Mildred L. Batchelder Award, given by the American Library Association to an American publisher for "the children's book considered to be the most outstanding of those books originally published in a foreign language . . . and subsequently published in the United States."

Of FRIEDRICH and I WAS THERE, Dr. Richter says: "They are in fact autobiographical books. A large part of the population in Köln (Cologne), the town of my birth and my adolescence, was Jewish so that involuntarily, I witnessed the described events. The autobiographical character of I WAS THERE is indicated in the introductory note to the book."

Dr. Richter is a social psychologist who is the author of a number of professional publications in his field. He has done extensive research on the aged, and his interests in literature, history and current events have made him a frequent guest on radio and TV shows throughout Europe. Married and the father of three girls and one boy, he and his family make their home in Mainz, Germany.

ABOUT THE TRANSLATOR

Edite Kroll was born and raised in Germany and completed her education at Cambridge University in England and the *Alliance Française* in Paris. Long involved with children's literature, she has worked as an editor of juvenile books both in England and the United States. Now a free-lance editor/translator, Mrs. Kroll lives in Cumberland Center, Maine, with her husband, writer Steven Kroll.